THE BUMPER BOOK OF
KERRYMAN JOKES

Des MacHale

MERCIER PRESS

MERCIER PRESS
Douglas Village, Cork, Ireland
www.mercierpress.ie

Trade enquiries to COLUMBA MERCIER DISTRIBUTION,
55a Spruce Avenue, Stillorgan Industrial Park, Blackrock, Dublin

ISBN 1 85635 470 9

10 9 8 7 6 5 4 3 2 1

Mercier Press receives financial assistance from
the Arts Council/An Chomhairle Ealaíon

Printed and Bound by J. H. Haynes & Co. Ltd, Sparkford

A businessman hired a Kerry girl as his personal secretary but after a week noticed that she was no longer answering the phone. When asked for an explanation she said, 'What's the point? Nine times out of ten it's for you anyway.'

☺   ☺   ☺

Have you heard about the Kerry clairvoyant?
    He could look into the past.

☺   ☺   ☺

What does a Kerryman take with him to a cock fight?
    His duck.

☺   ☺   ☺

How do you know if a Kerry cock fight is rigged?
    The duck wins.

☺   ☺   ☺

A tourist passing through Kerry saw a loaf of bread sitting in the middle of the road, so he took it to the local garda station.
    He was told to hold onto it for thirty days and if nobody claimed it he could keep it.

☺   ☺   ☺

Kerry undertakers have just gone on an all-out strike. However, they are going to provide a skeleton service to handle emergencies.

☺   ☺   ☺

Two Kerryman made the Irish bobsleigh team for the Winter Olympics. However, they refused to take part in the heats until the track was gritted.

☺   ☺   ☺

Where would you find a Kerryman the day his boat comes in?
    Waiting at the airport.

☺   ☺   ☺

Have you heard about the Kerryman who used to take two hot water bottles to bed with him?
    It was just in case one of them sprang a leak.

☺   ☺   ☺

A Kerryman went up to Dublin on a day trip and was stopped by an American tourist who asked him what time it was.
    'I'm sorry,' said the Kerryman, 'I'm a stranger here myself.'

☺   ☺   ☺

A Kerryman has just been made Minister for Defence.
    His first task is to have de fence painted.

☺   ☺   ☺

A Kerryman was out for a ride on his donkey when the animal took fright, bolted and finally wound up with one of his hind legs caught in one of the stirrups.
    'Hold on a minute,' said the Kerryman. 'If you're getting on then I'm getting off.'

☺   ☺   ☺

Sticker seen on a Kerryman's car:
'Thank you for not laughing at this car.'

☺ ☺ ☺

What organisation has the following uniform: – A purple three-cornered hat with a green feather, scarlet tunic, canary yellow trousers, and white sequined boots?
   The Kerry secret service.

☺ ☺ ☺

A Kerryman walked into a post office and asked the girl behind the counter, 'What's the postage on a letter bomb?'

☺ ☺ ☺

A Kerryman applying for a job was asked by his prospective employer how many honours in his Leaving Certificate he had.
   'Fifty-three,' said the Kerryman.
   'You must be joking,' said the employer.
   'Well, you started it,' said the Kerryman.

☺ ☺ ☺

Two Kerrymen had been marooned on a desert island for several weeks and were running out of food and water.
   'We've had it,' said the first, 'nothing can rescue us now.'
   'Hold on,' said the second, 'we're saved, here comes the *Titanic.*'

☺ ☺ ☺

Want to get your name in print? Just send €50 to the new Kerry Directory of Confidence Trick Victims.

Have you heard about the Kerry video recorder?

It records the programmes you don't want to see and shows them when you are out of the house.

☺   ☺   ☺

A Kerryman went to Liverpool and was having a drink with his friends.

'Try to be sophisticated,' his friends told him, 'and when the barman asks you what you are having, say you'll have a lager and lime.'

'Right,' said the Kerryman, and proceeded to place his order.

'How much lime, sir?' asked the barman.

'About a shovelful,' said the Kerryman.

☺   ☺   ☺

A Kerryman was asked in a survey what he thought of the United Nations. 'It was fine,' he replied, 'until they started letting all those foreigners into it.'

☺   ☺   ☺

Have you heard about the new Kerry waterproof watch?

It comes filled with water and you can't get it out no matter how hard you try.

☺   ☺   ☺

Sign in a Kerry grocery store:
'Mothers are requested not to leave their babies sitting on the bacon slicer because we are getting a little behind with our orders.'

☺   ☺   ☺

We find the man who stole the mare not guilty.

We return a verdict of guilty against the unknown murderer who killed O'Sullivan.

Not guilty, but we recommend that he doesn't do it again.

Unanimous – nine to three.

Your honour, we are all of one mind – insane.

Not guilty – if he'll promise to emigrate.

We find the prisoner guilty and recommend that he be hanged, and we hope it will be a warning to him.

Judge to defendant: you may leave the courtroom a free man with no stain on your character except for the fact that you were acquitted by a Kerry jury.

We the jury would have given anything to have seen the fight.

☺   ☺   ☺

'A rainbow,' a Kerryman once declared, 'is not really an optical illusion, it only looks like one.'

☺   ☺   ☺

Have you heard about the Kerry businessman who returned his dictaphone and complained that it spoke with a Kerry accent?

Some Famous Kerrymen

Seán D'Olier – Famous for hanging from the ceiling.

Rick O'Shea – Famous for banging his head off the wall.

Eoghan Cash – The famous Kerry bankrupt.

Nick McGuinness – Famous for stealing other people's pints.

Mick Dawire – The famous Kerry electrician.

Seán Ó Súilamháin – The famous one-eyed Kerryman.

Pat Pending – The famous inventor from Kerry.

Don Diggin – The famous retired Kerry undertaker.

Phil McCavity – The famous Kerry dentist.

Evel O'Kneivel – He jumped over twenty motorbikes in a double-decker bus.

P. King and his wife Nan King – The famous Chinese Kerry couple.

Cowjack – The famous Kerry detective.

The Jap of Dunloe – The famous yellow-skinned Kerryman.

Nelly Savalas – The famous bald Kerrywoman.

Nick O'Teen – Introduced tobacco into Kerry.

SOME KERRY INVENTIONS

The inflatable dartboard for campers

Ejector seats for helicopters

Contact lenses with frames

Peep-toed galoshes

A floodlit sundial for night use

The silent alarm clock (which won the Nobel prize)

A parachute that opens on impact

A unisex maternity hospital

A cure for which there was no known disease

A plan to straighten the Leaning Tower of Pisa

Boil-in-the-bag cornflakes

A bar of soap with a hole in the centre to avoid having awkward little pieces left at the end

Cow pâté

☺   ☺   ☺

Sign in a Kerry beauty parlour:
'Ears pierced while you wait.'

☺   ☺   ☺

Two Kerrymen were walking down the street when one turned to the other and said, 'Look, there's a dead pigeon.'

'Where? Where?' said the second Kerryman, looking up at the sky.

☺   ☺   ☺

The parish priest in a little Kerry church was astonished to see a Kerryman doing the Stations of the Cross starting at the fourteenth and working backwards.

'That's not the way to do it,' said the parish priest, 'you've got to start at number one.'

'I thought there was something wrong all right,' said the Kerryman, 'He seemed to be getting better.'

☺   ☺   ☺

At a Kerry court case the judge said: 'Will the defendant please rise,' and one of the jurymen stood up.

'How come,' asked the judge, 'that you the defendant are on the jury?'

'I don't know,' said the Kerryman sheepishly, 'I thought I was kinda lucky.'

☺   ☺   ☺

Have you heard about the new game that's all the rage?

It's called Kerry Roulette – you simply bang your head against the wall six times, once very hard.

☺   ☺   ☺

A Kerryman walked into a bar and said to the barman, 'Give me a Martinus.'

'Surely you mean Martini, sir,' said the barman.

'Look,' said the Kerryman, 'if I want two, I'll ask for them.'

What happens when you peel a Kerry onion?

It makes you laugh.

☺   ☺   ☺

Have you heard about the Kerryman who died as a result of too much drink?

He was run over by a Guinness lorry.

☺   ☺   ☺

A Kerryman went up to Dublin for the All-Ireland Final and had a drop too much to drink on the Saturday night before the match. At about eleven o'clock he hailed a taxi and said to the driver, 'Drive me round St Stephens Green four hundred times, and step on it, I'm in a hurry.'

☺   ☺   ☺

HAVE YOU HEARD ABOUT THE KERRYMAN ...

Who used to wear a wig with a big hole in the middle?

He figured that if he looked bald people wouldn't realise he was wearing a wig.

Who saw a notice 'Please Mind the Step' in a shop?

He had to wait over an hour until someone else came along to mind it for him.

Who ate fifty packets of cornflakes?

He died of sunstroke.

Whose library was burned down?

Both books were destroyed and one of them hadn't even been coloured in.

Who went to a drive-in movie?
    He didn't like the show so he slashed the seats.

Who won the Nobel Prize for Agriculture?
    He was simply a man outstanding in his own field.

Who tried to blow up a bus?
    He burned his lips on the exhaust pipe.

Who drove his car into a lake?
    He wanted to dip the headlights.

Who drove his car over a cliff?
    He wanted to test the airbrakes.

☺   ☺   ☺

Sign in a Kerry toilet:
'Please do not eat the large Polo mints in the urinals.'

☺   ☺   ☺

Two Kerrymen were sitting in a pub.
    'Could you tell me the time?' asked the first.
    'Certainly I could,' said the second.
    'Thank you very much,' said the second Kerryman.

☺   ☺   ☺

Have you heard about the Kerry operatic tenor who was given seventeen encores at La Scala, Milan?
    The audience wouldn't let him leave the stage until he sang the piece properly.

☺   ☺   ☺

A company selling hair restorer once received the following testimonial from a Kerryman:–

Dear Sir,

Before using your hair restorer I had three bald patches. Now I have only one.

☺ ☺ ☺

Have you heard about the Kerryman who went to England and made big money there but wound up in jail?

The money was just a quarter of an inch too big.

☺ ☺ ☺

Kerry businessman: 'Where's my pencil?'
Secretary: 'It's behind your ear, sir.'
Kerry businessman: 'Look, I'm a busy man, which ear?'

☺ ☺ ☺

A Kerryman was speaking in a debate about the evils of slaughtering animals. 'How about those people who kill pigs,' he thundered, 'despite the fact that they give us such lovely bacon.'

☺ ☺ ☺

A ninety-two-year-old Kerryman and his ninety-year-old wife have just applied for a divorce. They were waiting for their children to die.

☺ ☺ ☺

Have you heard about the Kerry salesman who only got two orders in an entire week?

They were 'get out' and 'stay out'.

A Kerryman wrote a postcard to his girlfriend and wrote above her address 'Private and Confidential'.

☺   ☺   ☺

EXAMINATION TO BECOME A KERRYMAN

Instructions to Candidates

Answer only one question at a time.

Do not attempt to write on both sides of the paper at the same time.

Slide Rules OK.

Candidates found cheating will be given extra marks for initiative.

Extra marks for creative spellings.

No point copying from the student in front of you – he probably knows less than you do.

Time allowed – until the cows come home.

1. Who won the First World War? Who came second?

2. Explain in one sentence Einstein's Theory of Relativity OR Write your name in block capitals.

3. Is this a question?

4. Name the odd man out: The Pope, The Chief Rabbi, The Yorkshire Ripper, The Archbishop of Canterbury.

5. What is the number of this question?

6. At what time is the nine o'clock news broadcast?

7. Spell each of the following words: dog, cat, pig.

8. Write a tongue twister three times quickly.

9. There have been two kings of England named Charles. The first was Charles the First – name the other one.

10. Magellan made three trips around the world and died on one of them. Which one?

11. Ignore this question completely.

12. 'The Kerryman joke is the highest form of art' (Shakespeare). Discuss.

A Kerryman rang the post office and said, 'The cord of my telephone is too long. I nearly tripped on it the other day. Would you mind giving it a pull at your end?

☺   ☺   ☺

Have you heard about the Kerry air force recruit who jumped out of a plane at 20,000 feet without a parachute because he was only practising?

☺   ☺   ☺

Two Kerrymen were pilot and co-pilot of a jumbo jet. One day coming into Shannon airport they overshot the runway and had to take the aircraft back up again and circle the airport. It happened a second time but at the third attempt, with a superhuman effort, the plane was brought to a halt only six inches from the grass edge.

'Do you know,' said the first Kerryman, 'that's the shortest runway I've ever come across.'

'Well, it's the widest one I've ever come across,' said the second Kerryman.

☺   ☺   ☺

A Kerryman went to college and got BA, MA and PhD degrees in literature but couldn't get a job, so he went to England to work on the buildings. The foreman decided to give him a test before he would take him on.

'What's the difference between a joist and a girder?' he asked.

'Well,' said the Kerryman, 'Joyce wrote *Ulysses* and Goethe wrote *Faust*.'

☺   ☺   ☺

Two Kerrymen were at a bingo session and one of them kept looking over the other's shoulder and telling him when his numbers were being called.

The second Kerryman got annoyed and said, 'Look, why don't you fill in your own card?'

'I can't,' said the first Kerryman, 'it's full.'

☺   ☺   ☺

Two Corkmen and a Kerryman were about to be shot by firing squad so they decided to try and divert their executioners and escape in the resulting confusion.

'Air-Raid,' shouted the first Corkman, and made his escape as the guards took cover.

'Avalanche,' shouted the second Corkman and he too got away.

'Fire,' shouted the Kerryman.

☺   ☺   ☺

HOW ABOUT ...

The Kerry fire extinguisher factory?
    It was burned to the ground.

The Kerry tadpole?
    He turned into a butterfly.

The Kerry ghost?
    He didn't believe in people.

The Kerry mosquito?
    He caught malaria.

The Kerry Gemini man?
    He presses a button and his watch disappears.

The Kerry mafia?
They threaten not to beat people up if they don't pay them money.

The Kerry nurse?
She used to wake patients up to give them their sleeping tablets.

The Kerry expedition to climb Everest?
They ran out of scaffolding thirty feet from the top.

The Kerry Institute for Advanced Studies?
It teaches fractions and long division.

The Kerry dwarf who was five feet tall?
He claimed he was the tallest dwarf in the world.

The Kerry turkey?
He kept looking forward to Christmas.

The Kerry fatted calf?
He said 'O goody, here comes the Prodigal Son.'

☺   ☺   ☺

SOME KERRY WILLS

I leave everything to myself.

I leave all my money and possessions to the doctor who will pull me through my final illness.

Then there was the Kerryman who didn't make any will at all because he thought it would be a dead giveaway to his relatives.

To my eldest son I leave the farm and to my second son I leave my seat in the Dáil.

I wish to be buried at sea – his son was drowned digging the grave.

☺   ☺   ☺

A *sign seen in Kerry:*
'For Sale
Tombstone
Bargain to anyone named Murphy.'

☺   ☺   ☺

A HINT OF GAELIC

What's a biafran?
    A Kerryman who goes to Mass twice on Sundays.

What's an oscillator?
    A Kerryman who eats donkeys.

If Blarney Castle could talk, what would it say?
    Póg mo stone.

Have you heard about the Kerryman who had a relapse of measles?
    It was a case of Arash Arís.

Bualadh bos is a crash between two Bus Éireann double-deckers.

What would you call an Indian draper living in Kerry?
Mahatma Geansaí.

Why did the Kerryman visit the RTE newsroom?

He wanted to know where they got all the ideas for the news.

☺   ☺   ☺

Have you heard about the Kerry Isaac Newton?

The apple tree fell on him and broke his neck.

☺   ☺   ☺

Then there was the Kerryman who lost his job and was replaced by a pocket calculator.

☺   ☺   ☺

Why did the Kerryman stop using egg shampoo?

The hen kept falling off his head.

☺   ☺   ☺

Have you heard about the Kerry cricket match that was cancelled because both sides showed up wearing the same colours?

☺   ☺   ☺

A dead Kerryman was smiling in his coffin.

His wife explained to a friend, 'He's smiling because he died in his sleep and he doesn't know he's dead yet. He's dreaming he's still alive, so when he wakes up and finds he's dead the shock will kill him.'

☺   ☺   ☺

Have you heard about the latest Kerry invention?
A hairdryer which works under water.

☺ ☺ ☺

Notice in a Kerry golf club:
'Trousers may now be worn by ladies on the course – but they must be removed before entering the clubhouse.'

☺ ☺ ☺

THICKSILVER

What's your name?
Stop the lights.

Name two days of the week that begin with the letter 'T'.
Today and tomorrow.

What was Hitler's first name?
Heil.

What's the best way to prevent forest fires?
Cut down all the trees.

Can you tell me the nationality of Napoleon?
Course I can.
Correct!

☺ ☺ ☺

How many kinds of pedestrian crossings are there?
Two ... Those who make it and those who don't.

☺ ☺ ☺

Who was born in a stable and has millions of followers?
  Arkle.

Why do surgeons wear masks over their faces?
  So that if the patient dies no one will know who did it.

What creature eats the least?
  The moth – he just eats holes.

Who invented the Aspirin?
  Mother Mary Aikenhead.

Who were Adam and Eve's children?
  That's a trick question – Adam and Eve had no children.

What was Gandhi's first name?
  Goosey Goosey

What do the letters AIB stand for?
  Artificial insemination by a bull.

Why is a giraffe's neck so long?
  It has to be because his head is so far away from his body.

To which family does the whale belong?
  I don't know, no family living near me has one anyway.

In anatomy, where is the lumbar region?
  Is it in the north of Canada?

How many degrees in a circle?
  How big a circle are you talking about?

What is meant by General Amnesty?
  He was the commander of the allied forces during the war.

What goes green, amber, red, green, amber, red?
   A packet of fruit gums.

What is backgammon?
   It's a sort of rasher.

Name two TV programmes about potatoes.
   Chips and Mash.

☺   ☺   ☺

Never make a task of pleasure as the Kerryman said as he dug his mother-in-law's grave only three feet deep.

☺   ☺   ☺

Please ring bell for porter – why can't the porter ring the bell for himself?

☺   ☺   ☺

Soon after the Department of Agriculture introduced its premium bull scheme, a Kerryman hired the best bull in the country to service his cows. After nearly a month the bull had not been returned, so the department dispatched an inspector hotfoot to Kerry to see what the situation was. He found the bull pulling a plough round a field, the Kerryman whipping him along and shouting, 'Get along outa that, ye bugger ye, that'll teach you there's more to life than romance'.

☺   ☺   ☺

Sign in a Kerry barbers:
'We pay 10 cent for every time the barber's hand slips and he draws blood – some customers leave here with a handsome profit.'

SOME KERRY GRAFFITI

John Lennon killed JR

Elvis is still dead

I'm a Kerryman and prowd of it

Thank God I'm an Atheist

There's no point voting in the elections – The government always wins anyway

Support the Kerry left-handed chess championships

Keep Kerry tidy – Dump your rubbish in Cork

Abolish hire education

Help stamp out quicksand

☺   ☺   ☺

A consortium of Kerry businessmen have put together twenty million euro to raise the *Titanic*.
They've just raised the iceberg.

☺   ☺   ☺

Have you heard about the Kerryman who got a BA degree in Computer Science and Art?
He got a job painting computers.

☺   ☺   ☺

One Kerryman met another who was wearing a beautiful 500 euro mohair suit though it was a bit on the big side for him. 'That's a lovely suit,' said the first Kerryman, 'where did you buy that?'

'Actually,' said the second Kerryman, 'I didn't buy it at all – it was a present from the wife. I came home early from work one day and found it lying on the bed.'

☺   ☺   ☺

Have you heard about the enthusiastic Kerry guard who once summoned a motorist for having bald tyres?

The case was dismissed because it turned out the fellow was driving a steamroller.

☺   ☺   ☺

What is the definition of an optimist?

A penniless Kerryman ordering oysters in a posh hotel in the hope that he can pay the bill with the pearls.

☺   ☺   ☺

Kerryman jokes are not new. In 1423 the inhabitants of a little Kerry village built a ten-foot wall around the village to keep the Plague out.

☺   ☺   ☺

Letter from a Kerryman's mother:

Dear Son,

I haven't written to you since the last time I wrote. I'm writing this very slowly because I know you can't read very quickly. If you don't get this letter write and let me know at once. When you write there is no need to put our address on the envelope as the postman knows well enough where we live by now.

We went to Ballybunion for a week this summer and it only rained twice – the first time for three days and the second time for four days. Your father has a great new job where he is over five hundred men – he's cutting the grass in the local cemetery. Your aunt Mary has just had her appendix taken out and a new washing machine installed. Your uncle Tom, the one who drank ten glasses of liver salts every day for the last forty years, died last week. We had to beat his liver to death with a stick. The people next door are keeping pigs in their backyard. We only got wind of it yesterday. Your uncle Frank who works in the brewery was drowned last week in a big vat of beer. He didn't have a painful death though because he got out three times to go to the gents.

I'm sending you three socks by parcel post as you said in your last letter that you had grown another foot since you left home. I'm also sending you a new jacket and to save weight I have cut off all the buttons. You'll find them in the pocket.

May God protect you
from your loving Mother

P.S. I would have enclosed five euro but I had already sealed the envelope.

☺   ☺   ☺

HOW ABOUT ...

The Kerry picket?
  It went on strike.

The Kerry jellyfish?
  It set.

The Kerry tug-of-war team?
    They were disqualified for pushing.

The Kerry grandmother who went on the pill?
    She didn't want any more grandchildren.

The Kerry helicopter pilot who felt a bit cold?
    He turned the fan off.

The Kerry explorer who paid €10 for a sheet of sandpaper?
    He thought it was a map of the Sahara Desert.

The Kerryman who was taking his driving test?
    He opened the door to let the clutch out.

The Kerryman who bought a black and white dog?
    He figured the licence would be cheaper than for a coloured one.

The Kerry kidnapper?
    He enclosed a stamped addressed envelope with the ransom note.

The Kerry Soldier?
    He went into Fota zoo, shot six gorillas and freed the ostriches.

The eighty-year-old Kerryman who married an eighty-five-year-old wife?
    He wanted someone to answer the rosary for him. They spent the entire honeymoon trying to get out of the car.

The Kerry comedian who quit the stage?
    People kept on laughing at him.

The Kerry sailor who claimed the Irish navy was much better than the British navy?

When he was in the Irish navy he could go home for his tea every evening.

The Kerryman who spent an hour in a big store looking for a cap with a peak at the back?

The Kerryman who was stranded for an hour in a super-market when the escalator broke down?

The Kerry plastic surgeon?

He sat near the fire and melted.

The Kerry schoolboy who used to play truant from school on Saturday?

The Kerry boy who swallowed a fifty-cent piece because it was his lunch money?

☺ ☺ ☺

Kerry doctor: 'Have you taken this patient's temperature?'
Kerry nurse: 'No. If it's missing, it wasn't me who took it.'

☺ ☺ ☺

SOME KERRY INVENTIONS

A new kind of bread.

So light that a pound of it weighed only four ounces.

The world's strongest glue.

But the inventor couldn't get the top off the bottle.

A new pill guaranteed to cure loss of memory.
    But the inventor couldn't remember what it was for.

A mechanical weather forecaster.
    Consisting of a piece of old rope. When the rope moves over and back it's windy and when the rope gets wet it's raining.

A cure to help you forget all about amnesia.

A wooden substitute for marble.
    It was so realistic that it sank as soon as you put it in water.

Inflammable Asbestos.
    That can be disposed of by burning.

A roll-bar for motor boats.

Burned-out lightbulbs for darkrooms.

A new cure for seasickness.
    Sit under a tree.

☺   ☺   ☺

First Kerry poet: 'How are things with you?'
Second Kerry poet: 'Not too good, I can't get my latest poem finished. I've been looking for a single word for two weeks.'
First Kerry poet: 'How about a fortnight?'

☺   ☺   ☺

Sign in a Kerry auctioneers:
'The highest bidder to be the purchaser – Unless somebody bids more.'

Have you heard about the Kerryman who has stopped putting his clock forward every year?

It kept falling off the mantelpiece.

☺   ☺   ☺

One Saturday the *Irish Examiner* announced that it was increasing its price by ten cent on the following Monday.

A Kerryman went out and bought all the copies he could find on Saturday.

☺   ☺   ☺

Have you heard about the Kerryman who had a false wisdom tooth fitted?

☺   ☺   ☺

A Kerryman and his wife went on holiday to London and stayed at the Savoy Hotel. When they returned the wife remarked to a neighbour, 'What upset Dinny most was that the manager of the hotel had never even heard of him. Sure in Kerry he's world famous.'

☺   ☺   ☺

A Kerryman was once charged with attacking a Corkman with a razor.

He was acquitted because he hadn't plugged it in.

☺   ☺   ☺

A Kerryman went to his psychiatrist and told him he was worried because he had a collection of over ten thousand CDs and couldn't stop buying them.

'There's nothing to worry about,' said the psychiatrist, 'I

like to play CDs myself.'

'Oh, I don't play them,' said the Kerryman, 'I just collect the holes in the middle.'

☺   ☺   ☺

'You are charged,' said the judge to a Kerryman, 'with having wilfully, feloniously and with malice aforethought appropriated to your own use and behoof a certain article, to wit, a bovine quadruped – the said quadruped having been wrongfully and feloniously abstracted by you from the estate of one Daniel Murphy on or about the fourth day of July, *Anno Domini* 1980, contrary to the law of the land. How do you plead?'

'Not guilty, your honour,' said the Kerryman, 'all I did was steal a cow.'

☺   ☺   ☺

How do you recognise ...

A Kerry pirate?
He's got a patch over each eye.

A Kerry bride?
She's the one with the white wellies.

A Kerry bath?
It's got taps at both ends to keep the water level.

A Kerry business executive?
He's the one wearing the pinstripe wellies.

A Kerry string quartet?
They stop every few minutes to clear the saliva from their instruments.

A Kerryman's matched luggage?
Two plastic bags from the same supermarket.

A Kerry card sharp?
He plays the one card trick.

A Kerry hippy?
Flared wellies.

A Kerry aircraft?
It's got outside toilets.

A topless Kerry restaurant?
It's got no roof.

A Kerry streaker?
He's fully clothed.

A Kerry submarine?
It's got half doors.

☺   ☺   ☺

A Kerryman got out of jail digging a tunnel and climbing over a two-hundred foot wall. So he rang the jail and asked if he could speak to himself, prisoner 36129.

The jailer said, 'I'll check, sir,' and came back in a few minutes and reported that that particular prisoner's cell seemed to be empty.

'Hurrah,' said the Kerryman, 'I've escaped.'

☺   ☺   ☺

First Kerryman: 'What's Mick's other name?'
Second Kerryman: 'Mick who?'

Have you heard about the Kerryman who used to eat nothing except paper clips?

His doctor had put him on a staple diet.

☺   ☺   ☺

A Kerryman had a drop too much to drink so he was taken to the station and asked to walk the white line. He refused to do it without a safety net.

☺   ☺   ☺

How do you ask a Kerryman for change?

Say, 'Can you give me two tens for a five?'

If he complains say, 'I was only joking, give me back my two tens, here's your five.'

☺   ☺   ☺

How do you recognise a Kerry hippy?

He keeps plastic marijuana plants in his greenhouse.

☺   ☺   ☺

One morning a Kerryman got a parcel in the post marked in large red letters 'Handle with care'. Excitedly he opened it and inside he found a handle.

☺   ☺   ☺

First Kerry workman: 'Have you that hammer, Mick?'
Second Kerry workman: 'I have.'
First Kerry workman: 'Where have you it?'
Second Kerry workman: 'I have it lost.'

Who joined the navy?
  He was given a job as a deckhand on a submarine.

Who joined the 'Save Energy' campaign?
  He stopped working.

Who became a director in the film business?
  He got a job as a cinema usher.

Who went playing water polo?
  His horse was drowned.

Who set fire to his jacket?
  Because he wanted a blazer.

Who put his television set in the oven?
  He wanted a TV dinner.

Who tried to get a no claims bonus of his life insurance?

Who cheated Iarnród Éireann?
  He bought a return ticket to Dublin and never went back.

Who damaged his health drinking milk?
  The cow fell on him.

Who couldn't understand how people always seemed to die in alphabetical order?

☺   ☺   ☺

Sign outside a Kerry garage:
'Our attendants are filling fine. Tank you.'

First Kerry snake: 'Are we a poisonous variety of snake?'
Second Kerry snake: 'I don't know. Why do you ask?'
First Kerry snake: 'I've just bitten my tongue.'

☺   ☺   ☺

Have you heard about the Kerry stork?
He used to deliver butter to maternity hospitals.

☺   ☺   ☺

Have you heard about the Kerryman's pet mosquito?
It was so tame it used to eat out of his hand.

☺   ☺   ☺

Two Kerrymen joined the army during the Second World War and were fighting in the trenches for the first time. To encourage them, their sergeant promised them a pound for every German they killed. One afternoon one of them was woken up from his nap by the other shouting, 'They're coming, they're coming!'

'Who's coming?' said the other.

'The Germans, that's who.'

'How many are there?'

'About a hundred thousand.'

'Begorra,' said the Kerryman reaching for his rifle, 'our fortune's made.'

☺   ☺   ☺

Comment at a Kerry funeral:
'If that man was alive today, he'd turn in his grave to see some of the people who turned up at his funeral.'

☺   ☺   ☺

A Kerryman was out walking one day when he spotted a leprechaun so he captured him and demanded three wishes.

'Right,' said the leprechaun, 'what's your first wish?'

'I'd like a purse full of gold,' said the Kerryman, 'that no matter how much you take out of it, it will never be empty.'

'Right,' said the leprechaun and gave it to him.

The Kerryman grabbed it and tried it out and was delighted to see that it worked.

'For my second and third wishes, I'll have two more of those purses.'

☺   ☺   ☺

HOW MANY KERRYMEN DOES IT TAKE ...

To launch a ship?

1001 – One to hold the bottle of champagne and a thousand to bang the ship against it.

To milk a cow?

24 – One to hold each teat and twenty to lift the cow up and down.

To hang a picture?

30 – One to hold the picture, one to hold the screw and twenty-eight to turn the wall around.

To change a light bulb?

100 – One to actually change the light bulb and ninety-nine to share the experience.

To carry out a kidnapping?

Ten – One to capture the kid and nine to write the ransom note.

To wash an upstairs window?
    Two – One to wash the window, one to hold the ladder.

To wash a downstairs window?
    Four – One to wash the window, one to hold the ladder and two to dig a hole for the ladder.

☺   ☺   ☺

Two signs seen on the same pole in Kerry:
'Gentlemen's Toilet'
'Limit Two Tons'

☺   ☺   ☺

THE KINGDOM STRIKES BACK

Why are Corkmen so constipated?
    They hate to part with anything.

Why do Claremen have scratched faces?
    From trying to eat with knives and forks.

What do you get if you cross a Sligoman with a gorilla?
    A mentally deficient gorilla.

Why did the Mayo fisherman stay unmarried?
    He couldn't find a girl who had worms.

What do you get if you cross a Dubliner with a boomerang?
    A dirty smell you can't get rid of.

What do you call a Corkman who marries a gorilla?
    A social climber.

How do you brainwash a Tipperaryman?
    Fill his wellingtons with water.

What do you call a pimple on a Kilkennyman's rear end?
    A brain tumour.

Have you heard about the Mayoman who had a brain transplant?
    The brain rejected him.

☺ ☺ ☺

SOME KERRY INVENTIONS

A cure for wheatgerm

Non-stick glue

A new way to keep you from losing your hair – sew a name tag inside your hairpiece

A new cure for hiccups – hold your breath and count to a million

Motorway bowling

The crossed line – invented by Alexander Graham Sheehy

A hernia transplant

An out-patient morgue

Dehydrated water for desert explorers

A washing machine for disposable nappies

The million euro sweepstake – one euro to the winner every year for a million years

A foolproof way of avoiding parking tickets – take the windscreen wipers off your car

Green golf balls

☺   ☺   ☺

HAVE YOU HEARD ABOUT THE KERRYMAN …

Who never bought a suit with two pairs of trousers?
　He felt too hot wearing two pairs of trousers.

Who swallowed a pillow?
　He felt a little down in the mouth.

Who got 100% in his exam?
　20% in English; 30% in Irish; 40% in mathematics; 10% VAT.

Who had a drink problem?
　He couldn't afford all he was drinking.

Who bought a carpet in mint condition?
　It had a hole in the middle.

Who stayed up all night studying for a blood test?

Who got a new boomerang for Christmas?
　It took him six months to throw his old one away.

Who thought the charge of the light brigade was his ESB bill?

Who thought free speech meant not having to pay your telephone bill?

Who wrote a first-class novel?
　You know the way kids write in first class!

Who came home one night and found his house locked?

He borrowed a ladder, climbed in an upstairs window and found a note from his wife in the kitchen saying, 'the key is under the doormat and your salad is in the oven.'

Who went to a fire sale and bought a fire?

Who wrote to the income tax people and told them he didn't want to join their club?

Who put a packet of Daz on his television set because he did not have any ariel?

Who took nothing for a headache because he heard that nothing acts faster than Anadin?

Who hijacked a submarine?

He demanded a million euro ransom and a parachute.

☺   ☺   ☺

An important businessman was staying in a little Kerry hotel and the receptionist asked him if he would like a call in the morning.

'Certainly not,' he snapped. 'I wake at seven o'clock sharp every morning.'

'In that case,' said the receptionist, 'would you mind calling the porter?'

☺   ☺   ☺

HAVE YOU HEARD ABOUT THE KERRYMAN WHO THOUGHT ...

Cyclamates were a husband and wife on a tandem?

Hard water was another name for ice?

Champagne was French for 'false window'?

The English Channel was BBC television?

Johnny Cash was a sort of pay toilet?

That if he fell in love he would lose his appetite?
He was right – for tea he used to have eighteen slices of bread; now he only eats seventeen.

Radio Activity was what went on in RTE?

☺   ☺   ☺

Sign by a postbox in a Kerry post office:
'For letters too late for the next delivery.'

☺   ☺   ☺

THICKSILVER

In astronomy what's another name for a star with a tail?
Mickey Mouse.

What's the difference between electricity and lightning?
You have to pay for electricity.

What's the connection between 1916 and 1798?
Adjoining rooms in a Kerry hotel.

How do you tell the difference between a baby boy and a baby girl?
A baby boy wears blue bootees and a baby girl wears pink bootees.

How do you tell the difference between a toadstool and a mushroom?

Eat it – if you die it's a toadstool and if you live it's a mushroom.

What are your parent's names?

Mamma and Dadda.

Why do storks have such long legs?

If their legs were any shorter they wouldn't reach the ground.

How do you spell 'Tipperary'?

Do you mean the town now or the county?

What do you call a male bee?

A wasp.

What is the Ayatullah famous for?

He founded the ceilí band.

Who was the mythical creature, half man, half beast?

Buffalo Bill.

What rugby player has been capped most times for Ireland?

A. N. Other.

☺   ☺   ☺

A Kerryman bought one of the fantastic new Japanese mini bubble cars but it didn't work out very well.

Dogs kept wetting the windows.

☺   ☺   ☺

A Kerryman fell into shark-infested waters but survived because he was wearing a t-shirt with 'Cork for the Sam Maguire Cup' on it – not even the sharks would swallow that.

☺ ☺ ☺

A Kerryman went into a butcher's shop and saw an electric fan in its protective wire grill for the first time.

'That's a very lively bird you have in that cage,' he said to the butcher.

☺ ☺ ☺

Have you heard about the Kerry beggarman who was standing at a street corner with a hat in each hand?

Business was so good he explained that he had opened a branch office.

☺ ☺ ☺

A Kerryman was being tried on a serious offence.

'You say you left the county in 1976,' said the prosecuting counsel, 'and returned in 1979. What were you doing in the interim?'

'Never set foot in the place,' said the Kerryman.

☺ ☺ ☺

A Kerryman owned an optician's shop and one Friday afternoon at about a minute to closing time a fellow walked in with a broken pair of glasses and asked if they could be fixed as he needed them for the weekend.

'Sorry,' said the Kerryman, 'we're just closing but I could board them up for you until Monday.'

☺ ☺ ☺

A Kerryman was doing a test to become a policeman.

'How far is it from Cork to Dublin?' he was asked.

'I don't know,' said the Kerryman, 'but if that's going to be my beat, I don't want the job.'

☺   ☺   ☺

HAVE YOU HEARD ABOUT THE KERRYMAN WHO THOUGHT ...

Manual labour was a Spanish trade union official?

Slim panatella was a country and western singer?

Chou-en-lai was Chinese for bed and breakfast?

Yoko Ono was Japanese for one egg please?

A discotheque was a Cork traffic warden?

A metronome was a dwarf who lived in the Paris underground?

A stalagmite was a midget who lived in a German concentration camp?

Copper nitrate was overtime pay for policemen?

Hertz van rental was a Dutch artist?

A P45 was a revolver?

Pas de deux was French for father of twins?

☺   ☺   ☺

Sign in a Kerry opticians' window:
'If you can't read this notice come in and have your eyes tested – you may need glasses.'

☺   ☺   ☺

Have you heard about the ship that set sail from Kerry with a cargo of yo-yos?

It sank two hundred and thirty-seven times.

☺   ☺   ☺

Two Kerrymen were boasting to each other how dumb their sons were. 'Let me show you how bad my son Mick is,' said the first. 'Come here, Mick,' he said, calling him in. 'Here's a euro, now go into town and buy me a Rolls Royce.' Off went Mick to town.

'That's nothing,' said the second Kerryman. 'Wait until you see my son Dinny. Come here, Dinny; now go into town to Sullivans' pub and see if I'm there.' So off went Dinny.

On the way to town Mick and Dinny met and began to boast about how dumb their fathers were.

'Take my old man,' said Mick. 'He just sent me into town with a euro to buy a Rolls Royce, and every fool knows the salesrooms are closed today.'

'That's nothing,' said Dinny. 'My old man is really the limit. He's just sent me into Sullivan's pub to see if he's there. Couldn't he have just picked up the phone by his elbow and found out for himself in a second?'

☺   ☺   ☺

Have you heard about the Kerryman who was sentenced to transportation for life in Tasmania in 1773? He came to a sticky end because he tried to tunnel his way out of the prison ship.

A rather mean tourist arrived in Kerry and asked if he could have a bed for the night for €15.

'Right,' said a Kerry hotelier, anxious to please.

'If I give you another euro will you throw in breakfast as well?' asked the skinflint.

'Right,' said the Kerryman, raising his eyes to Heaven.

At about six o'clock in the morning the tourist was awakened by the door opening suddenly and a loud thump on the floor.

'What was that?' he cried in alarm.

'Breakfast being thrown in,' smiled the Kerryman.

☺ ☺ ☺

A Corkman holidaying in Kerry lost his post office savings book. A few weeks later it was handed to the gardaí with €500 extra deposited in it.

☺ ☺ ☺

THE KINGDOM STRIKES BACK

How do you break an Offalyman's finger?
  Kick him in the nose.

What's the most popular kind of marmalade sold in Waterford?
  Thick cut.

Newspaper headline – Bed collapses in Sunday's Well, 43 Corkmen hurt.

The EU has just given €1,000 million to build three new looney bins. One is in Rome, one is in Brussels and they're putting a roof over Dublin.

What's the world thinnest book?
The Book of Carlow Intellectuals.

Have you heard about the raffle where first prize was a week in Longford and second prize was two weeks in Longford?

What does a Louthman think when he gets diarrhoea?
He thinks he's melting.

How do you know if a Wicklowman is in love?
If he washes his feet more often than once a month.

What's the difference between a Wexfordman and a bucket of manure?
The bucket.

How do you save a Galwayman from drowning?
You don't know? Good.

Have you heard about the Limerickman who thought he was a great wit?
He was half right.

What's the latest thing in air pollution?
The Roscommon parachute club.

Have you heard about the Cork goalkeeper who was so depressed after a six-goal defeat by Kerry that he threw himself under a bus?
He missed and the bus went under his body.

What do you call a dead Dubliner?
A jack in the box.

What did God say when he made his second Meathman?
Gee, I must be losing my touch.

How do you tell the age of a Cavanman?
   Cut off his head and count the rings.

What's the difference between a Mayoman and a ham sandwich?
   A ham sandwich is only half an inch thick.

How do you keep Leitrimmen out of your house?
   Hide the key under a bar of soap.

How do you recognise a Kerryman in Croke Park?
   He's the one holding the Sam Maguire cup!

What do you call an intelligent Mayoman?
   Very, very lucky.

Why do Tipperarymen always carry a little rubbish in their pockets?
   Identification.

Have you heard about the Corkman who had an inferiority complex?
He thought other people were nearly as good as he was.

What's the difference between a Dublin wedding and a Dublin wake?
   One less drunk.

A Kerryman had a clever little dog that he took to the Munster football final each year. After the match the dog would bark out Kerry's winning score and clap his little paws together. A reporter from the *Irish Examiner* asked him what the dog did when Cork won.
   'I don't know,' said the Kerryman, 'I've only had him ten years.'

What's blue and white and slides down the table?
  The Dublin football team.

Why do Donegalmen have big noses?
  Donegalmen have such big fingers.

What is gross ignorance?
  144 Corkmen.

What does a Clareman do when he stops drinking?
  He belches.

Why are Kerrymen jokes so simple?
  So Mayomen can understand them.

What's blue and white and floats upside down in the Liffey?
  A Dubliner caught telling Kerryman jokes.

What's a Cork barbecue?
A fire in a garbage pail.

A Donegalman rushed into a barber's shop with a pig under
his arm.
  'Where did you get that?' asked the barber.
  'I won him in a raffle,' said the pig.

☺   ☺   ☺

WHAT DO YOU CALL ...

A Kerryman chasing a garbage truck?
  A galloping gourmet.

A Kerry garda sitting up a tree?
  A special branch man.

A Kerryman under a wheelbarrow?
    A mechanic

A Kerryman who rides his bicycle on the pavement?
    A psychopath.

A Kerryman travelling to Cork with a wheelbarrow?
    A thrill-seeker.

A brick on a Kerryman's head?
    An extension.

☺   ☺   ☺

A Kerryman told his little boy to go down to the chemist shop and buy half a pound of cockroach powder. 'But,' he warned him, 'don't let on to the chemist what it's for.'

The little boy bought the powder and then asked the chemist, 'is this stuff good for cockroaches?'

'No,' said the chemist, 'it kills them stone dead.'

☺   ☺   ☺

A Kerryman once claimed that Kerry had the best climate in the country except for the fact that the weather ruined it.

☺   ☺   ☺

The first time a Kerryman saw a toupee in a shop window he said, 'isn't it amazing how they can get hair to grow on that thing but not on your head.'

☺   ☺   ☺

Have you heard about the Kerry snake?
    He fell in love with a coil of rope.

A Kerry priest was preaching to his congregation in the middle of the nineteenth century.

'Drink is the cause of all your problems,' he thundered. 'It makes you angry, it makes you hate your landlords, it makes you shoot at your landlords, and worst of all, it makes you miss.'

☺   ☺   ☺

A West Cork farmer went to a fair in Kerry with his beautiful ivory-handled whip, whose name he pronounced 'Wup'. However, he lost his wup and was going from pub to pub asking everyone if anybody had seen his wup. In one pub one little Kerryman nudged another and said, 'Did oo hear fwat he called his fip?'

☺   ☺   ☺

If a Kerryman dials a wrong number what does he say to the person who answers the phone?

'You fool, you've got the wrong number.'

☺   ☺   ☺

A Kerryman was kissing his girlfriend passionately when her father suddenly burst into the room. He grabbed the Kerryman by the throat and shouted, 'What were you doing to my daughter?'

'I was only whispering into her mouth, sir,' said the Kerryman.

Sign in a Kerry church:
'Closed on Sundays.'

☺   ☺   ☺

A Kerryman on an oil-rig?
  He's the one throwing crusts of bread to the helicopters.

A Kerryman Santa Claus?
  He's carrying a bag of Easter eggs.

A forged Kerry €5 note?
  Look for the words 'illegal tender'.

A Kerry zebra?
  He's called 'Spot'.

A Kerryman in a car-wash?
  He's the one sitting on his motor-bike.

A Kerry camel?
  He's always thirsty.

A Kerry woodworm?
  He's dead on top of a brick.

A Kerry Formula One driver?
  He makes a hundred pit stops – three for fuel, four for tyre changes and ninety-three to ask for directions.

A well-mannered Kerryman?
  He doesn't blow his soup – he fans it with his cap.

A Kerryman's toilet roll?
  Look for the instructions printed on every sheet.

☺   ☺   ☺

During a recent petrol crisis a Kerryman was charged with siphoning the air out of the tyres of a car.

Clever Kerrymen however survived the crisis by putting a brick in their petrol tank.

☺ ☺ ☺

Have you heard about the Kerry hedgehog?

It fell in love with a hairbrush.

☺ ☺ ☺

A Kerryman got a job as a doorman in a big building. He managed very well with the Push and Pull signs but he was seen struggling with his fingers under a door marked Lift.

☺ ☺ ☺

A Kerryman was captain of a jet and one day he made the following announcement to his passengers over the public address system. 'Ladies and gentlemen, sorry for the long delay in take-off. I'm delighted to announce that we haven't got a bomb on board as we first feared. At least, if we have, we haven't been able to find it.'

☺ ☺ ☺

A Kerryman got a job as a chauffeur to a duchess and gave every satisfaction as a driver. However, she noticed that he was a little careless about his appearance and in particular that he didn't seem to shave every day, so she decided to drop a few hints.

'James,' she said one morning to him casually, 'how often to you think one should shave?'

'Well, ma'am,' he replied slowly, 'with a light growth like yours, I'd say about once every three days.'

A Kerryman was asked to join the Save Energy campaign by not carrying heavy, unnecessary weights in the boot of his car. He decided to leave his car jack at home because he did not use it very often.

☺   ☺   ☺

HAVE YOU HEARD ABOUT THE KERRYMAN ...

Who became a tap dancer?
  He got washed down the sink.

Who tried to iron his curtains?
  He fell out the window.

Who took his trousers off when the doctor told him to strip to the waist?

Who claimed he caught a fish so big that the photograph alone weighed twenty pounds?

Who sent his kids to a school for emotionally disturbed teachers?

Who wasn't superstitious in case it brought him bad luck?

Who got a pair of cuff links for Christmas?
  He had his wrists pierced.

Who only had three children because he heard that every fourth child born is Chinese?

Who failed to get into the gardaí because the minimum height was 5' 8" and he was 5' 9"?

Who thought that publishers had entered into a conspiracy against him because twenty of them returned the manuscript of his first novel?

Who refused to pay going into the art gallery because he was only looking?

☺ ☺ ☺

Sign in a Kerry dance hall:
'Ladies and gentlemen welcome
Regardless of sex.'

☺ ☺ ☺

A Kerryman was in charge of a hospital for the disabled and one day he was showing a millionaire round the place in the hope of getting a large donation from him. So he took him into a ward where there was a man with no arms. 'That's dreadful,' said the millionaire. 'Look, here's a cheque for €50,000.' The Kerryman thought he would squeeze a little more money out of him, so he took him into a ward where there was a man with neither arms nor legs. 'That's terrible,' said the millionaire. 'I'll increase that to €100,000.'

The Kerryman decided to squeeze just a little more money out of his benefactor, so he took him to a ward where there was a bed with just a single tooth lying on the pillow.

'Oh my God,' gasped the millionaire, 'is that all that's left of the poor fellow?'

'Worse still,' said the Kerryman, 'he's having it out tomorrow.'

☺ ☺ ☺

What does a Kerryman think when he sees his underarm hair?

He thinks the stuffing is coming out.

A Kerryman was drinking too much, so his local parish priest persuaded him to join the Pioneer Total Abstinence Association. About a week later the parish priest observed the Kerryman staggering out of a pub.

'I thought you were a pioneer now,' said the parish priest.

'I am,' said the Kerryman, 'but not a bigoted one.'

☺   ☺   ☺

A Kerryman went to the doctor to get some medicine as he wasn't feeling very well.

'This is pretty strong stuff,' said the doctor, 'so take some the first day, then skip a day, take some again and then skip another day and so on.'

A few months later the doctor met the Kerryman's wife and asked her how he was.

'Oh he's dead,' she told him.

'Didn't the medicine I prescribed do him any good?' asked the doctor.

'Oh the medicine was fine,' she replied. 'It was all that skipping that killed him.'

☺   ☺   ☺

Why are there so many great Kerry pianists and so few great Kerry violinists?

Have you ever tried balancing a pint of porter on a violin?

☺   ☺   ☺

HAVE YOU HEARD ABOUT THE KERRYMAN WHO THOUGHT ...

Tonic solfa was something you put in a drink?

A spirit level was a breathaliser for carpenters?

VAT 69 was the pope's telephone number?

Bacteria was the rear entrance to a café?

Et cum spiritu 20 was the bishop of Dublin's telephone number?

Capital punishment meant living in Dublin?

Sherlock Holmes was a block of flats?

An innuendo was an Italian suppository?

Interpol would send a parrot abroad for you?

A barbecue was a line of people outside a hairdressers?

The AAAA was an association for drunks who drive?
So he joined and when he got drunk he rang them up and they towed him away from the bar.

Syntax was money paid to the government by wrongdoers?

Coq au vin was chicken that fell off the back of a lorry?

Plato was a Greek washing-up liquid?

☺   ☺   ☺

THE KINGDOM STRIKES BACK

Why do Dubliners keep their mouths open all the time?
They're so lazy it saves them having to open their mouths when they want to yawn.

How do you get forty Corkmen into a mini?
Tell them it's going to Dublin.

How do you get them out again?

Tell them they're sharing the petrol.

What is black and frizzled and hangs from the ceiling?

A Galway electrician.

How does a Dubliner keep flies out of his kitchen?

He dumps a load of manure in his living-room.

Why do birds fly upside down over Kerry?

To save all they've got for Cork.

How do you know if a Meathman is lying?

If his lips are moving.

Have you heard about the Corkman who was wrong only once in his life?

That's when he thought he had made a mistake.

What's the difference between a Kildareman and his photograph?

The photograph is fully developed.

A new police inspector was assigned to Kerry, so before the announcement of his appointment was made, he slipped down to Kerry, incognito, to see what the situation was like. One night, near midnight, he met the local garda and asked him if he knew any place where he could get a drink after hours.

'Don't worry,' said the garda, 'I'll look after you.' And he took the shocked new inspector to a pub where they had a whale of a time in the company of dozens of Kerrymen.

At about 4 a.m. the inspector turned to the garda and said, 'what would your sergeant say if he could see you now?'

'He'd say wasn't I the cute lad to be drinking with the new inspector,' smiled the Kerry garda.

Advertisement in a Kerry newspaper:
'Passport for Sale: Owner going abroad.'

☺   ☺   ☺

Have you heard about the Kerryman who got sick all over the floor of a Dublin art gallery?

He was offered €35,000 for it.

☺   ☺   ☺

How do you recognise a Kerryman in Las Vegas?

He's the one playing the stamp machine.

☺   ☺   ☺

A Kerryman was boasting about the ring he had bought for his wife.

'It's got four diamonds, three rubies and half a dozen sapphires … missing.'

☺   ☺   ☺

A Kerryman went into a bar with two sophisticated friends.

'I'll have a Martini,' said the first, 'with an olive in it please.'

'I'll have a brandy,' said the second, 'and put a cherry in it please.'

'I'll have a pint of porter,' said the Kerryman, 'and put an onion in it.'

☺   ☺   ☺

Have you heard about the Kerryman who got a job as a tea-bag drier for Iarnród Éireann?

☺   ☺   ☺

How do you recognise a Kerryman's best socks?

The ones with the fewest holes.

☺   ☺   ☺

A Kerryman was asked how many honours he had obtained in his Leaving Cert.

'Three,' he replied, 'Applied Mathematics and Pure Mathematics.'

☺   ☺   ☺

Have you heard about the Kerryman who returned to Ireland during the famine to open a fish and chip shop?

☺   ☺   ☺

Two Kerrymen were out walking together when they saw a lorry pass by laden with grassy sods of earth for the laying of a lawn.

'Do you know Mick,' said one of them to the other, 'if I ever get rich that's what I'll have done – send away my lawn to be cut.'

☺   ☺   ☺

Kerry Road Sign:
'This is the wrong road to Dublin
Do not take this road.'

☺   ☺   ☺

Sign in a Kerry shop:
'No dissatisfied customer is ever allowed to leave this shop.'

☺   ☺   ☺

Have you heard about the Kerry addict who quit the drug scene?

He tried sniffing coke but the bubbles kept going up his nose.

☺ ☺ ☺

A Kerry barman was closing up one night when he found a customer flat out under a table so he propped him up against the bar. When he turned round he found the fellow had slid onto the floor again so he picked him up, searched his pockets and found his name and address. So he put him in his car, drove him home, and carried him up to the front door. To ring the doorbell, he propped him up against the wall and found that he again slid down on the ground. As he tried to lift him up again, the fellow's wife opened the door and said, 'Oh thank goodness you've brought him home – but where's his wheelchair?'

☺ ☺ ☺

In a little Kerry village the coroner was summing up in a suicide case before a jury of twelve Kerrymen.

'If you believe beyond reasonable doubt,' he told them, 'that the deceased did shoot himself with a gun, then it is your duty in law to return a verdict of *felo de se*.'

The jury was out about four hours and when they returned the foreman said, 'We agree that the deceased did shoot himself with a gun, but if the coroner claims he fell in the sea we return a verdict of accidentally drowned.'

☺ ☺ ☺

A Kerryman was in court charged with parking in a restricted area. The judge if he had anything to say in his defence.

'They shouldn't put up such a misleading notice,' said the Kerryman, 'It said "Fine for parking here".'

Two American ladies had just been driven round the Lakes of Killarney by a silver-tongued little jarvey for over four hours. As they paid him they said, 'We'd love to give you a tip but there is a notice on your jaunting car saying "Tipping Forbidden".'

'God help your sense,' smiled the Kerryman, 'Tipping Forbidden! So was eating apples in the Garden of Eden.'

☺   ☺   ☺

A Kerryman went for an X-ray and was immediately rushed to hospital for a hole-in-the-heart operation. Then they discovered it was only a Polo mint in his shirt pocket.

☺   ☺   ☺

HOW DOES A KERRYMAN …

Amuse himself?
   He writes P.T.O. on both sides of a piece of paper.

Make a Venetian blind?
   He throws acid in his eyes.

Make anti-freeze?
   He hides her woollen nightie.

Make an old German whine?
   He stands on his toes.

Make a Swiss roll?
   He pushes him down the Alps.

Make a Maltese cross?
   He bites his finger.

Cure water on the brain?
  With a tap on the head.

Cure water on the knee?
  With pumps and drainpipe trousers.

Tear a telephone directory in two?
  Page by page.

☺ ☺ ☺

A Kerryman went to confession and confessed his sins.
  'You are forgiven,' said the priest. 'Now for your penance say three Hail Marys.'
  'But I only know one,' said the Kerryman.

☺ ☺ ☺

A Kerryman went into a bar and the barman said, 'What are you having sir?'
  'Thank you very much,' said the Kerryman, 'I'll have a pint.' So the barman pulled him a pint and asked for the appropriate amount of money.
  'Hold on,' said the Kerryman. 'You asked me what I was having, so this should be a free drink.'
  'Get out of here,' said the barman angrily, 'and don't come back.'
  About a month later the Kerryman walked into the same bar with the same barman behind the counter.
  'Look,' said the barman, 'I thought I told you to get out and stay out.'
  'That's a nice way to treat a new customer,' said the Kerryman, 'I've never been in here in my life before.'
  'I'm terribly sorry sir,' said the barman, 'I mistook you for someone who looks remarkably like you. You must have a double.'

'Certainly,' said the Kerryman, 'I'll have a double brandy.'

Have you heard about the Kerry boxer who never won any of his fights?

Every time an opponent knocked him down he remembered what his mother had told him so he counted to ten before getting up and hitting him back.

☺   ☺   ☺

A Kerryman got a job in a big house as a servant but one afternoon he knocked over a priceless Ming vase and broke it into little pieces.

'Good Heavens,' said his employer, 'do you realise what you have done? That vase was over a thousand years old.'

'Thank goodness,' said the Kerryman, 'it wasn't a new one.'

☺   ☺   ☺

Members wanted by the Kerry fencing club – new blood is always welcome.

☺   ☺   ☺

Have you heard about the Kerryman who went into a draper's shop and asked for some of the new terminal underwear?

☺   ☺   ☺

CAUSES OF DEATH ON SOME KERRY DEATH CERTIFICATES ...

He didn't die of anything serious.

Had never been fatally ill before.

Went to bed feeling very well but woke up dead.

An act of God under very suspicious circumstances.

Cause of death unknown as he died without the aid of a doctor.

[Of a hated landlord found with twenty bullet wounds, ten fatal, ten non-fatal] – Lead poisoning.

He died of a Tuesday.

The patient died in a state of perfect health.

[Of a man found dead with thirty stab wounds and twenty bullet wounds] – The worst case of suicide ever seen in the country.

☺   ☺   ☺

Have you heard about the Kerryman who set out to walk around the world?

He was drowned just off Valentia Island.

☺   ☺   ☺

Two Kerrymen went to South America where they were caught up in a revolution. They were captured and sentenced to death by firing squad. As they were about to be shot, one of them asked for a blindfold but was refused.

'How come,' he protested, 'that the two fellows who were shot just before us were given blindfolds?'

'Look,' said the other Kerryman, 'don't make trouble.'

☺   ☺   ☺

Have you heard about the Kerryman who invented a new shockproof, waterproof, rustproof watch?

It was for people who wanted to tell the time when they were drowning.

☺ ☺ ☺

An old Kerry army sergeant wasn't feeling very well so he went to the doctor and had a check-up.

'When did you last have a drink?' the doctor asked him. '1958,' said the Kerryman.

'That's a long time without a drink,' said the doctor.

'It certainly is,' said the Kerryman. 'It's nearly 2130 now.'

☺ ☺ ☺

Have you heard about the Kerryman charged with breaking into Áras an Uachtaráin?

He gave himself away by signing the Visitors' Book.

☺ ☺ ☺

A Kerryman was a lighthouse-keeper for forty years and every hour on the hour a big bell on the lighthouse rang out the time. One night he went to bed at midnight having heard the clock ring out twelve times. He went to sleep but at one o'clock the bell failed to ring, and there was complete silence. The Kerryman sat bolt upright in his bed and said, 'What was that?'

☺ ☺ ☺

Have you heard about the Kerryman who became a hero when his house was flooded?

He went back in to rescue the goldfish.

☺ ☺ ☺

A Kerryman had a severe pain in his head so he went to the doctor who examined his brain. But the doctor found nothing.

☺   ☺   ☺

Why ...

Do Kerry dogs have flat faces?
  From chasing parked cars.

Do you never get ice in your drink in Kerry?
  The fellow with the recipe emigrated.

Do Kerry fish swim backwards?
  To keep the water from getting into their eyes.

Does a Kerryman smile when struck by lightning?
  He thinks he's having his photograph taken.

Did the Kerryman put his wife under the bed?
  He thought she was a little potty.

Do Kerrymen smile so much?
  Their false teeth are too big for them.

Does a Kerryman read the obituary column in his newspaper every morning?
  To see if he's still alive.

Do Kerrymen never mention the number 288?
  It's too gross.

Do Kerry workers never get tea breaks?
  It takes too long to retrain them afterwards.

Do Kerrymen make poor card players?
    Every time they pick up a spade they spit on their hands.

☺   ☺   ☺

Sign in a Kerry restaurant:
'Closed for Lunch.'

☺   ☺   ☺

How do you recognise a bathing suit made in Kerry?
    Look for the label which says 'Dry Clean Only'.

☺   ☺   ☺

An Irish-speaking Kerryman went to Iraq where he was being questioned about his political opinions.
    'Do you support the Ayatollah?' they asked him.
    'Sea,' he replied, so they shot him.

☺   ☺   ☺

Two Kerrymen joined the RAF during the Second World War and were sent on a mission to drop bombs over Germany. As they flew over Berlin they were met by a burst of anti-aircraft guns, machine guns and chased by German aircraft.
    At the height of the action one of the Kerrymen shouted out 'Hurrah for de Valera.'
    'What on earth are you shouting out that?' asked the other Kerryman.
    'Wasn't it him that kept us out of the war?' said the first Kerryman.

☺   ☺   ☺

A tourist called at a hotel owned by a Kerryman and asked what his weekly rates were.

'I don't know,' said the Kerryman, 'nobody has ever stayed that long.'

☺   ☺   ☺

How do you recognise a Kerryman in a bus?

He's the one sitting in the back seat because he thinks he's getting a longer ride.

☺   ☺   ☺

A Kerryman's shop was burgled one night so he called the police.

'Thank goodness it wasn't last week it happened,' he said to a policeman.

'Why is that, sir?' asked the policeman.

'Well,' said the Kerryman, 'I'd have lost a colossal amount of money; but this week I was having a sale and everything was marked down 50%.'

☺   ☺   ☺

Sign outside a Kerry barbers:
'Special offer
Haircuts 50 cent this week only
One per customer only.'

☺   ☺   ☺

A Kerryman's cat was feeling out of sorts so he called in the vet.

'There's noting really the matter with your cat,' said the vet. 'It's all perfectly natural, she's going to have kittens.'

'That's impossible,' said the Kerryman, 'she's a prize-winning cat and I've never let her out of my sight for a moment. She's never been near a tom cat in her life.'

'How about him over there?' asked the vet, pointing to a big tom cat sitting on a couch smiling to himself.

'Don't be ridiculous,' said the Kerryman, 'that's her brother.'

☺   ☺   ☺

Advertisement from the newspapers:
'Wanted urgently – new members for a suicide club in the Kerry area.'

☺   ☺   ☺

How do you sell a twenty-pound hammer to a Kerryman?
Tell him it costs only €10.

☺   ☺   ☺

Have you heard about the latest Kerry invention?
It's a digital sundial.

☺   ☺   ☺

A customer went into a shop owned by a Kerryman and asked to buy some mustard.

'I don't have any in the shop,' said the Kerryman, 'but I have some in the store; come with me and pick out the kind of mustard you want.'

As they went through the store the customer couldn't help noticing bag after bag of salt on the shelves.

'You must sell an awful lot of salt,' he remarked to the Kerryman.

'I sell very little salt,' said the Kerryman, 'but the fellow who sells me salt, boy, can he sell salt.'

☺   ☺   ☺

Have you heard about the Kerryman who got rid of his vacuum cleaner because he felt it was only gathering dust?

☺ ☺ ☺

HOW DO YOU RECOGNISE …

A Kerryman who owns a Volkswagen?
He has a fifteen-foot starting handle.

A Kerryman's central heating system?
Lagging jackets on the radiators.

A Kerry racing cyclist?
Stabilisers on his bicycle.

A Kerry physical fitness fanatic?
He rolls his own cigarettes.

A passionate Kerryman?
He takes the cigarette out of his mouth when kissing a girl.

A Kerryman's cordless razor?
A piece of sandpaper.

A Kerry mugger?
He gives his victims business cards in case they are ever in the neighbourhood again.

A Kerry tortoise?
His shell has been recalled.

A Kerry water skier?
He is being towed by a rowboat.

Kerry identical twins?
They can't tell each other apart.

☺   ☺   ☺

Sign in a Kerry post office:
'Pens will not be provided until people stop taking them away.'

☺   ☺   ☺

Have you heard about the Kerryman who took a speed-reading course?
The first book he read afterwards was *War and Peace* and when asked what it was about he replied, 'It's about Russia.'

☺   ☺   ☺

A fellow went into a shop owned by a Kerryman and asked for some toilet paper.
'Sorry,' said the Kerryman, 'we have no summer novelties in stock at the moment.'

☺   ☺   ☺

There's a fantastic new act that's going down very well on the cabaret scene – a Kerryman who does volcano impressions. He fills his navel with talcum powder and coughs.

☺   ☺   ☺

One Kerryman was showing off his knowledge to another, so he asked him if he knew what shape the world was.
'I don't,' said the second Kerryman. 'Give me a clue.'
'It's the same shape as the buttons on my jacket,' said the first Kerryman.
'Square,' said the second Kerryman.

'That's my Sunday jacket,' said the first Kerryman. 'I meant my weekday jacket. Now what shape is the world?'

'Square on Sundays, round on weekdays,' said the second Kerryman.

☺   ☺   ☺

Have you heard about the Kerryman who thought that the *Cork Examiner* was a specialist employed in the wine industry?

☺   ☺   ☺

Have you heard about the Kerryman who took his girlfriend into the Tunnel of Love? They got down to work right away and by the time they came out they had developed three films.

☺   ☺   ☺

HOW ABOUT …

The Kerryman who was glad he wasn't born in Russia because he didn't speak a word of Russian?

The Kerry moon rocket that didn't quite make it?
    It ran out of turf.

The Kerry sheepdog trails where all ten dogs were found guilty?

The Kerryman who always drove with the handbrake on so as to be ready for emergencies?

The generous Kerry businessman who gave large amounts of money to charity but never signed the cheques because he wanted to remain anonymous?

The Kerry thrill-seeker who ate his after-eight mints at 7 o'clock?

The Kerryman who thought the Avon Lady was Shakespeare's wife?

The Kerryman who liked sandwiches?
     When he wasn't very hungry, a pound of butter between two loaves; when he was hungry a bull between two bread vans.

The Kerry skier who kept trying to get his ski-pants on over his skis?

The superstitious Kerry boxer who attributed his success to the fact that he always carried his lucky horseshoe in his glove?

The Kerryman who took up yoga to help him quit smoking?
     Now he can smoke standing on his head.

The Kerry cat burglar who stole only cats?

The Kerryman who fooled the income tax people by dropping dead?

The Kerryman who was so ugly a Halloween mask company bought up the rights to his face?

The Kerryman who got a job where all he had to do was press a button to start a machine at 8 o'clock and to press it again to stop it at 5 o'clock? He quit because he wanted a less technical job.

The Kerryman who thought an asset was a little donkey?

A Kerryman's description of a well-known Corkman:

'I'm not saying he's crazy enough to be put in a looney bin, but on the other hand, if he was in one I don't think they would let him out.'

☺ ☺ ☺

A Kerrywoman was telling a friend that she had over fifty goldfish.

'Where do you keep them?' the friend asked.

'In the bathtub,' she replied.

'But what do you do when you want to take a bath?'

'I blindfold them,' said the Kerrywoman.

☺ ☺ ☺

Have you heard about the Kerry swimming gala that was cancelled because the pool was waterlogged?

☺ ☺ ☺

Two Kerry farmers met one day at a fair.

'Tell me,' said the first, 'what did you give your mule when he had colic?'

'Turpentine,' said the second.

A few months later they met again.

'What did you say you gave your mule when he had colic?' asked the first.

'Turpentine,' said the second.

'Well I gave my mule turpentine, and he died,' said the first.

'So did mine,' said the second Kerryman, 'so did mine.'

☺ ☺ ☺

Sign on a Kerry lorry:
'No hand signals – Driver eating his Yorkie bar.'

A Kerryman was sentenced to be hanged, but saved his life by dying in prison.

☺ ☺ ☺

A Kerryman was in casualty ward of a hospital when he was visited by the Lady Mayoress of the city.

'Now my good man,' she asked him, 'where were you injured?'

'Well ma'am,' said the Kerryman, 'let me put it this way – if you had been injured where I had been injured, you would not have been injured at all.'

☺ ☺ ☺

A Kerryman went to a riding stable and hired a horse.

'Hold on for a moment,' said the assistant as he helped him on the horse, 'aren't you putting that saddle on backwards.'

'You don't even know which way I want to go.'

☺ ☺ ☺

How do you recognise a Kerryman in a shoe shop?

He's the one trying on the shoeboxes.

☺ ☺ ☺

A Kerryman called the police to complain about his neighbours. 'Come up here with me and listen to this,' he said to the sergeant, taking him upstairs into the bedroom and beckoning him to put his ear to the wall.

'I can't hear a thing,' said the sergeant.

'I know,' said the Kerryman, 'and it's been like that all day.'

☺ ☺ ☺

A Kerryman had just been found guilty of a serious crime and the judge asked him if he could pay anything at all towards costs which had also been awarded against him.

'Not a penny your honour,' said the Kerryman. 'Everything I own I've given to my lawyer and three of the jury.'

☺   ☺   ☺

First Kerryman: 'I've just bought one of those new silicon chip hearing aids – it's so small you can hardly see it.'
Second Kerryman: 'That's terrific – does it work well?'
First Kerryman: 'Half past seven.'

☺   ☺   ☺

A Kerryman joined the American air force and was making his first parachute jump. The instructor said 'When you jump out of the place shout "Geronimo" and pull the rip-cord.'

When the Kerryman woke up in hospital a few days later the first thing he said was 'What was the name of that Indian again?'

☺   ☺   ☺

Have you heard about the Kerryman who broke his leg smoking?

He throw his cigarette end down an open manhole and tried to step on it.

☺   ☺   ☺

Two Kerrymen went into a pub, ordered two glasses of water and proceeded to take out their lunch boxes.

'Hold on a minute,' said the barman. 'You're not allowed to eat your own food in here.'

So the two Kerrymen swapped lunch boxes.

Two Kerrymen were in a railway station for the first time and they ran in terror as a train came flying in.

'Do you know what I'm going to tell you,' said one to the other, 'if that thing had come sideways it would have killed the both of us.'

☺   ☺   ☺

Judge: 'The jury have found you guilty.'
Kerryman: 'I know they have but I'm sure your honour has too much intelligence to pay any attention to what that shower of rogues say.'

☺   ☺   ☺

What to do in Kerry

Go down to the station to watch a train coming in.

Go to see the local barber give haircuts.

Read the tombstones in the cemetery.

See the new bacon slicer in action in the grocery store.

Watch the local alcoholic have delirium tremens.

Watch the lifeguard rescue people form the carwash.

Watch cars being filled with petrol at the filling station.

Call to the local undertakers and ask if he has any empty boxes.

☺   ☺   ☺

Sign somewhere in Kerry:
'Please do not steal this notice.'
Next day it was gone!

☺   ☺   ☺

Have you heard the one about the Kerryman who got a pair of water-skis for Christmas?
He's still going around looking for a lake with a slope.

☺   ☺   ☺

What do you do to a one-armed Kerryman who is hanging from a tree?
Wave to him.

☺   ☺   ☺

In which month do Kerrymen drink the least?
February.

☺   ☺   ☺

Why did God create alcohol?
To stop Kerrymen from ruling the world.

☺   ☺   ☺

Why do Kerrymen like underwater swimming?
Because deep down underneath they are quite intelligent.

☺   ☺   ☺

What is the happiest five-year period of a Kerryman's life?
Junior infants.

Why did the Kerryman cut a hole in his umbrella?
    He wanted to know when it stopped raining.

☺　☺　☺

What is the best thing that ever came out of Kerry?
    The train to Dublin.

☺　☺　☺

Why do Kerry policemen have numbers?
    In case they get lost.

☺　☺　☺

Have you heard about the Kerryman who went to a mind reader?
    He got his money back.

☺　☺　☺

What happens when a Kerryman moves to Dublin?
    He decreases the level of intelligence in both counties.

☺　☺　☺

What is the capital of Kerry?
    About €250.

☺　☺　☺

Why do Kerry workers never go on strike?
    Nobody would notice the difference.

☺　☺　☺

What two Kerrymen didn't invent the aeroplane?
    The Wrong brothers.

☺   ☺   ☺

Why has Australia got all the kangaroos and Ireland got all the Kerrymen?
    Australia had the first choice.

☺   ☺   ☺

Why does a Kerryman put his budgie in a goldfish bowl?
    When he puts it in a cage the water keeps coming out.

☺   ☺   ☺

What do you call the shock absorbers in a Kerryman's car?
Passengers.

☺   ☺   ☺

What does a golfer get if he asks his Kerry caddie for a sand wedge?
    Corned beef in brown bread.

☺   ☺   ☺

How do we know that Santa Claus is from Kerry?
    There are two doors and ten windows in the average house and he goes down the chimney.

☺   ☺   ☺

At what Olympic events have Kerrymen won the most medals?
    Heading the shot and catching the javelin.

Why was the Kerryman walking down the road knocking down little old ladies and hitting children?

He was on his way to confession and didn't have enough sins to confess.

☺ ☺ ☺

How do you recognise a Kerry nudist colony?

Men have blue ribbons in their hair while women have pink ribbons in their hair.

☺ ☺ ☺

Have you heard about the Kerryman who owned a newspaper?

It cost him 90 cent.

☺ ☺ ☺

Who is the odd man out in the following list – Donald Duck, an intelligent Kerryman, the Archbishop of Canterbury and King Kong?

The Archbishop of Canterbury – all the others are fictitious characters.

☺ ☺ ☺

What do you see written on the front of a Kerry Mystery Tour bus?

Destination Cork.

☺ ☺ ☺

Why don't Kerrymen eat Smarties?

It's too much trouble peeling off the shells to get at the chocolate.

How do you sink a Kerry submarine?
   Put it in water.

☺   ☺   ☺

What happened to the Kerryman who bought washable wall-paper?
   He'd only washed it twice when it was stolen from the clothesline.

☺   ☺   ☺

What industrial action do Kerry circus employees take?
   A go-slow on the Wall of Death.

☺   ☺   ☺

Have you heard about the Kerryman who won the Tour de France?
   He set off on a lap of honour and wasn't seen for a month.

☺   ☺   ☺

How would you get a Kerryman to climb onto the roof of a pub?
   Tell him the drinks are on the house.

☺   ☺   ☺

What is top of the bestseller list in Ireland this month?
   Memoirs of a Kerry Kamikaze Pilot.

☺   ☺   ☺

How does a Kerryman cope with a gas leak?
   He puts a bucket under it.

How do you recognise a Kerry cuckoo clock?

Every ten minutes the cuckoo pops its head out and asks the time.

☺ ☺ ☺

What did the Kerryman do when he saw a sign 'Keep death off the roads'?

He drove his car on the footpath.

☺ ☺ ☺

Have you heard about the Kerrywoman who bought *The Joy of Sex* for her husband for Christmas?

He coloured it in.

☺ ☺ ☺

Where is cleanliness next to Godliness?

In a Kerry dictionary.

☺ ☺ ☺

How do you recognise a Kerry typist?

Every time the little bell on her typewriter rings she takes a tea break.

☺ ☺ ☺

What did the Kerry loan shark do when he lent out €10 million?

He immediately skipped town.

☺ ☺ ☺

Have you heard about the Kerryman who fed and starved his pigs on alternate days?

He wanted to sell them for streaky bacon.

☺ ☺ ☺

Have you heard about the Kerryman who bought a paper shop?

It blew away.

☺ ☺ ☺

Is there a Kerry equivalent of mañana?

Yes, but it conveys nothing like the same sense of urgency.

☺ ☺ ☺

What is a Kerry teacher's definition of an audiovisual aid?

Do you see this stick and do you hear what I'm saying?

☺ ☺ ☺

What did the Kerryman do when he found his clothes line was too short?

He moved his house back ten feet.

☺ ☺ ☺

Have you heard about the two Kerry astronauts who went for a space walk?

They slammed the door of the spacecraft and left the key inside.

☺ ☺ ☺

Why did the Kerryman go into a second-hand shop?

To buy one for his watch.

How do you recognise a Kerryman's motor car?
    Windscreen wipers on the inside.

☺   ☺   ☺

How do you make a Kerry cocktail?
    Take half a glass of whiskey and add it to another half a glass of whiskey.

☺   ☺   ☺

Have you heard about the Kerry athlete who did a hundred metres in five seconds while wearing his wellies?
    He fell over a cliff.

☺   ☺   ☺

What is lesson one in a Kerry driving school?
    How to open a locked car with a wire coat hanger.

☺   ☺   ☺

Why do all Kerry football grounds have TV screens?
    So the fans can see what is happening in their local bar.

☺   ☺   ☺

Why did the Kerryman fail his driving test?
    His car rolled forward on a hill start.

☺   ☺   ☺

Why did the Kerryman return the dictionary he had just bought to the bookshop?
    Because it didn't have an index.

What is the latest Kerry population control policy?
Shoot all the storks.

☺   ☺   ☺

What is the government warning on Kerry cigarette packets?
Smoking shortens your cigarettes.

☺   ☺   ☺

Have you heard about the Kerryman who was scared of heights?
He wouldn't go upstairs in a jumbo jet.

☺   ☺   ☺

Why does a Kerryman take a box of matches to bed with him?
To see if he's turned out the light.

☺   ☺   ☺

What is the definition of a smart Kerryman?
He's got an IQ.

☺   ☺   ☺

Why did Kerry's top organist quit?
His monkey died.

☺   ☺   ☺

What does the Kerry speaking clock say?
In precisely two seconds it will be nearly three o'clock.

☺   ☺   ☺

What is the title of the bestselling sex manual in Kerry?
Brace Yourself Bridget.

☺   ☺   ☺

How do you get rid of a Kerry car?
Cover it with rust remover.

☺   ☺   ☺

Why did the Kerryman go to London on his honeymoon, alone?
Because his wife had been to London before.

☺   ☺   ☺

Have you heard about the Kerryman who was invited to a housewarming?
He spent the whole night helping to insulate the attic.

☺   ☺   ☺

How do you recognise an hour-long Kerry sex video?
It's got one minute of sex followed by fifty-nine minutes of guilt.

☺   ☺   ☺

What is white and goes upwards?
A Kerry snowflake.

☺   ☺   ☺

Why did nineteen Kerrymen go to a film together?
Because they was a notice 'Under 18 Not Admitted'.

Why did the Kerryman rub liniment on his head?
    He was told it would make him smart.

☺   ☺   ☺

Have you heard about the Kerry farmer who went away for the weekend and forgot to unhitch one of his cows from the milking machine?
    When he returned he found that the cow had been turned inside out.

☺   ☺   ☺

How do you recognise a Kerry bullet-proof vest?
    It has a money back guarantee if it doesn't work.

☺   ☺   ☺

What is four miles long and has an IQ of forty?
    A Kerry Saint Patrick's Day Parade.

☺   ☺   ☺

How do you recognise a Kerryman with an electric razor?
    He's got the bathroom covered in foam.

☺   ☺   ☺

Why did the Kerryman return his typewriter to the shop?
    Because the keys weren't in alphabetical order.

What is a Kerry transistor?
    A nun who wears men's clothes.

☺   ☺   ☺

Have you heard about the Kerry rabbit who got caught by his leg in a trap?

He chewed off three of his legs but found he was still caught in the trap.

☺ ☺ ☺

Why did the Kerry spacecraft crash?

It ran out of peat.

☺ ☺ ☺

Why was the Kerryman pouring a gallon of Guinness down the toilet?

He was cutting out the middleman.

☺ ☺ ☺

How does a Kerryman lay underground telegraph cables?

First he digs thirty-foot holes for the telegraph poles.

☺ ☺ ☺

Have you heard about the latest Kerry invention for looking through solid walls?

It's called a window.

☺ ☺ ☺

What happened to the Kerry Humpty Dumpty?

The wall fell on him.

☺ ☺ ☺

Why did the Kerry goalkeeper never bother stopping the ball?

He thought that was what the net was for.

Why did the Kerry train driver lose his job?
  For overtaking.

☺   ☺   ☺

Why did the Kerrywoman move from Tralee to Dingle?
  She wanted to be nearer her son in New York.

☺   ☺   ☺

What is green and drives to Dublin in reverse?
  A Kerryman who knows the Highway Code backwards.

☺   ☺   ☺

What does a Kerryman give an underweight parrot?
  A packet of Pollyfilla.

☺   ☺   ☺

What happened to the Kerry Leaning Tower?
  It was straightened by a Kerry builder.

☺   ☺   ☺

What did the Kerry heart transplant patient do?
  He sent a get well card to the donor.

☺   ☺   ☺

What do you call a Kerryman driving a Mercedes?
  A joy-rider.

☺   ☺   ☺

What happened to the Kerry ice hockey team?
  They drowned during spring training.

What do you call a Kerryman sitting in his back garden?
  Paddy O'Furniture.

☺ ☺ ☺

Have you heard about the Kerry hurricane?
  It did €10 billion worth of improvements.

☺ ☺ ☺

Have you heard about the Kerryman who lost all his luggage
at Heuston Station?
  The cork came out.

☺ ☺ ☺

What happened to the Kerryman who tried to commit
suicide by taking a hundred aspirins?
  After he took two he began to feel better.

☺ ☺ ☺

Why did the Kerryman lose his job as a barman?
  He rinsed the ice-cubes in hot water and spent half an
hour looking for them afterwards.

How did the four-foot Kerryman join the army?
  He lied about his height.

☺ ☺ ☺

What do you call a Kerryman in a detached house?
  A squatter.

☺ ☺ ☺

How do you recognise a Kerry gourmet?
He hangs the mince for a few days before cooking it.

☺   ☺   ☺

How do you disperse a crowd of Kerrymen in New York?
Shout 'immigration'.

☺   ☺   ☺

How does a Kerry driver prepare for emergency stops?
He keeps the handbrake on all the time.

☺   ☺   ☺

Have you heard about the Kerryman who won a trip to Japan in a raffle?
He's still out there trying to win a trip back.

☺   ☺   ☺

How many Kerrymen does it take to change a light bulb?
Two. One says to the other, 'Could you switch the light on in here, Mick? It's so dark I can't see what I'm doing'.

☺   ☺   ☺

Why do Kerry policemen always travel in threes?
One who can read, one who can write, and the third a special branch man to keep an eye on two such dangerous intellectuals.

☺   ☺   ☺

Have you heard about the Kerry ventriloquist?
His dummy quit to find a new partner.

How do you make a Kerryman laugh on Monday morning?
    Tell him a joke on Friday evening.

☺   ☺   ☺

What do you call a Kerryman's open convertible?
    A skip.

☺   ☺   ☺

What do you call a Kerryman on a bicycle?
    A dope peddler.

☺   ☺   ☺

Have you heard about the Kerryman who started a protection racket?
    He threatened to beat people up if they paid him money.

☺   ☺   ☺

How do you recognise a posh Kerryman?
    He picks his nose with his little finger.

☺   ☺   ☺

Have you heard about the Kerryman who bought a tube of toothpaste with the stripes?
    He wound up with alternate red and white teeth.

☺   ☺   ☺

What did the Kerryman say when he saw the Eiffel Tower?
    They'll never get it off the ground.

☺   ☺   ☺

Have you heard about the Kerryman who locked his keys in his car?

It took him five hours to get his family out.

☺   ☺   ☺

What has an IQ of 144?

A gross of Kerrymen.

☺   ☺   ☺

What does a Kerry chiropodist have for breakfast?

Cornflakes.

☺   ☺   ☺

How do you recognise a Kerry brothel?

It has bunk beds.

☺   ☺   ☺

What were the last words of the Kerry gangster?

Who put that fiddle in my violin case?

☺   ☺   ☺

How do you get 100 euro from a Kerryman?

Ask him to lend you €200. Then say, 'Look, give me €100. Then you'll owe me €100, I'll owe you €100 and we'll be square.'

☺   ☺   ☺

Why didn't the Kerry miner have a light on his hat?

He was on the day shift.

What are old Kerry fire engines used for?
False alarms.

☺ ☺ ☺

What is the definition of frustration?
A Kerry garage mechanic with greasy hands and no steering wheel to wipe them on.

☺ ☺ ☺

What did the Kerryman say when he was asked if he was a Catholic?
It's bad enough being an alcoholic.

☺ ☺ ☺

Why did the Kerryman cross the road?
To get to the middle.
OK try again.
Why did the Kerryman cross the road?
Because it was the chicken's day off.

☺ ☺ ☺

What is compatibility for a Kerryman and his wife?
They both have headaches on the same night.

☺ ☺ ☺

Have you heard about the Kerryman who refused to buy a Japanese radio?
He said he wouldn't be able to understand a word it said.

☺ ☺ ☺

Why did the Kerryman sue the bakery?

He claimed that they forged his signature on hot cross buns.

☺   ☺   ☺

What is the difference between a Kerry drunk and a Kerry alcoholic?

A Kerry drunk doesn't have to attend all those meetings.

☺   ☺   ☺

What did the Kerryman say when he was told that the kangaroo was a native of Australia?

To think that my sister married one of them things.

☺   ☺   ☺

What do you call a Kerryman's car with twin exhausts?

A wheelbarrow.

☺   ☺   ☺

What is the biggest educational problem in Kerry?

Kindergarten drop-out.

Why didn't the Kerryman intervene when he saw an old lady struggling with four muggers?

He didn't know who had started it.

☺   ☺   ☺

How do you recognise a Kerry Rubik cube?

All the faces are green and it only takes a few minutes to solve.

Have you heard about the Kerryman who got a job with Manchester United?

He used to carry the team to away matches.

☺   ☺   ☺

What do you call a Kerryman's boomerang that won't come back?

A stick.

☺   ☺   ☺

What did the Kerry Goldilocks say?

Who's been sleeping in my porridge?

☺   ☺   ☺

Why did the Kerryman sew a label marked 'cotton' on his wool pullover?

He thought it would fool the moths.

☺   ☺   ☺

What did the Kerryman do when his wife had twins?

He went out with a shotgun looking for the other man.

☺   ☺   ☺

Have you heard about the Kerryman who crossed a dog with a tortoise?

It goes to the shop and brings back yesterday's newspaper.

☺   ☺   ☺

What is the greatest achievement of the Kerry electronics industry?

They made the world's largest microchip.

How do you recognise a Kerry ghost?

He jumps over walls.

☺   ☺   ☺

Have you heard about the Kerry streaker?

He was taken to court but they couldn't pin a thing on him.

☺   ☺   ☺

Why does a Kerry wake last three days?

To make sure the fellow is dead and not just dead drunk.

☺   ☺   ☺

What do you do if a Kerryman throws a pin at you?

Run like mad; he's probably got a grenade between his teeth.

☺   ☺   ☺

Why was the Kerryman reading a book called *How to Bring up Children*?

One of his kids had just fallen down a well.

☺   ☺   ☺

Why was the Kerryman confused?

He couldn't understand how he had only three brothers while his sister had four.

☺   ☺   ☺

What is the only part of a Kerryman's car that doesn't make a noise?

The horn.

What is reality to a Kerryman?

    An illusion created by a lack of alcohol.

☺   ☺   ☺

How does a Kerryman call his dog?

    He puts two fingers in his mouth and shouts 'Rover'.

☺   ☺   ☺

Have you heard about the Kerryman who completed a jigsaw in only six months?

    He was very proud because it said '4–6 years' on the box.

☺   ☺   ☺

Why is the average Kerryman like a lighthouse in the middle of a bog?

    He's brilliant but useless.

☺   ☺   ☺

What is the most accurate description of a Kerryman?

    He's just a machine for turning potatoes into human nature.

☺   ☺   ☺

How do you recognise a Kerry firing squad?

    They stand in a circle so as not to miss.

☺   ☺   ☺

How do you tell if the condemned man is from Kerry?

    He doesn't duck.

What did the Kerryman say when the judge gave him 250 years in prison?

If I hadn't a smart lawyer I'd have got life.

☺   ☺   ☺

What is the definition of a true Kerryman?

Someone who would trample over the bodies of a dozen naked women to reach a pint of Guinness.

☺   ☺   ☺

Why did the Kerry couple have a perfect marriage?

She didn't want to and he couldn't.

☺   ☺   ☺

Why did the Kerrywoman give up breast-feeding?

After two feeds she ran out of breasts.

☺   ☺   ☺

What is the most favoured Kerry sex position?

Woman underneath, man in pub.

☺   ☺   ☺

What is the most popular sport in Kerry?

Turning Guinness into urine.

☺   ☺   ☺

When the Kerryman lost his dog, why didn't he put an ad in the newspaper?

Because his dog couldn't read.

Why was the Kerryman jumping up and down on his way to work?

He had taken some medicine and forgotten to shake it beforehand.

☺   ☺   ☺

Why was the Kerryman watering only half of his lawn?

Because the weather forecast said there was a 50% chance of rain.

☺   ☺   ☺

Why were a hundred Kerry sailors drowned?

They were push-starting a submarine.

☺   ☺   ☺

Why do Kerrymen's cars have such small steering wheels?

So they can drive with handcuffs on.

☺   ☺   ☺

Where do Kerrymen go on holiday?

To a different bar.

☺   ☺   ☺

Why did the Kerrywoman stop breast-feeding her baby?

It hurt too much when she boiled her nipples.

☺   ☺   ☺

Why did the Kerryman refuse to accept a new telephone directory?

He hadn't finished reading the old one.

What did the Kerry couple do when their sex therapist told them that the best position was man on top and woman underneath?

They slept for two years in bunk beds.

☺ ☺ ☺

For what are Kerry surgeons famous?

The difficult operation of appendix transplant.

☺ ☺ ☺

Where do you look for Kerry wall-to-wall carpets?

All along the ceiling.

☺ ☺ ☺

Why did the Kerryman not drink his medicine after a hot bath?

By the time he had finished drinking the hot bath he hadn't room for any more.

☺ ☺ ☺

Why did the Kerry fisherman throw back a two-foot long fish?

His frying pan was only a foot wide.

☺ ☺ ☺

Have you heard about the Kerry doctor who was treating a patient for jaundice for over three years?

He suddenly found out the fellow was Chinese. Worse still, he cured him.

☺ ☺ ☺

Why do you never find salt cellars in Kerry?

It takes too long to fill them through the little hole in the top.

☺   ☺   ☺

What does a Kerryman get if he multiplies 314159 by 2718?

The wrong answer.

☺   ☺   ☺

Why did the Kerryman buy 37 tickets when going to the cinema?

Some fellow inside the door kept tearing them up.

☺   ☺   ☺

What did the Kerryman do when he saw a notice outside the police station 'Man wanted for armed robbery'?

He went in and applied for the job.

☺   ☺   ☺

Why did the Kerry one-man bus crash?

The driver was upstairs collecting fares at the time.

☺   ☺   ☺

What happens to a girl who goes out with a Kerryman for an evening?

Nothing.

☺   ☺   ☺

Why was the Kerryman disqualified from the walking race?

Because he won it two years running.

Why did the Kerry level crossing have one gate open and one gate closed?

They were half expecting a train.

☺   ☺   ☺

How do you tell a Kerryman joke to a Kerryman?

Very slowly.

☺   ☺   ☺

What are the secret plans for the Kerry rocket to the sun?

They're sending it at night.

☺   ☺   ☺

How are Kerry flights announced at the airport?

The next flight for Kerry will leave when the big hand is at the two and the little hand is at the six.

☺   ☺   ☺

Why do Kerrymen not use local anaesthetics?

They think the imported ones are better.

☺   ☺   ☺

Why did the Kerryman visit the famous Harley Street plastic surgeon?

To have his plastic bucket mended.

☺   ☺   ☺

What was the message received by the Kerry deep-sea diver?

Come up immediately, we're sinking.

Why did the Kerryman learn to cut his fingernails with his left hand?

In case he ever lost the right.

☺   ☺   ☺

Why did the Kerryman's rope have only one end?

Because he cut off the other end.

☺   ☺   ☺

What do you find on the bottom of Kerryman beer bottles?

Open Other End.

☺   ☺   ☺

How do you recognise a Kerry shoplifter?

He steals free samples.

☺   ☺   ☺

How does a Kerryman tell his twin sons Mick and John apart?

He puts his finger in Mick's mouth and if he bites him he knows it's John.

☺   ☺   ☺

Have you heard about the Kerryman who got a job as quality control officer in a banana factory.

They had to let him go because he kept throwing away all the ones that were crooked.

☺   ☺   ☺

Why was the Kerryman committing suicide with a rope round his waist?

When it was around his neck it was choking him.

Why did the Kerryman want a train ticket to Jeopardy?
    Because he heard that there were 500 jobs in jeopardy.

☺ ☺ ☺

How do you recognise a Kerry football referee?
    He plays extra time before the match in case there is fog.

☺ ☺ ☺

Why did the Kerry spider stop spinning webs?
    Because he lost his pattern book.

☺ ☺ ☺

How do you recognise a Kerry chocolate?
    It melts in your hand, not in your mouth.

☺ ☺ ☺

Why was the Kerryman pushing his bike to work?
    He was so late he didn't even have time to get on it.

☺ ☺ ☺

How do you recognise a Kerry sundial?
    It loses ten minutes a day.

☺ ☺ ☺

Why did the Kerryman think that TV programmes had improved greatly?
    His wife had rearranged the furniture and he was watching the fish tank.

☺ ☺ ☺

What did the Kerryman say when the doctor told him he had German measles?

But I've never even been to Germany.

☺   ☺   ☺

What is the best-selling game in Kerry at Christmas?

The one-piece jigsaw.

☺   ☺   ☺

When do Kerrymen find the one-piece jigsaw difficult?

When they lose the top of the jigsaw box with the picture on it.

☺   ☺   ☺

How do you recognise a superstitious Kerryman?

He won't work on any week with a Friday in it.

☺   ☺   ☺

What was the Kerryman studying at medical school?

Nothing – they were studying him.

☺   ☺   ☺

Who is ten feet tall and lives in Kerry?

Paddy Long Legs.

☺   ☺   ☺

How did the Kerryman bite himself on the forehead?

He stood on a chair.

☺   ☺   ☺

How do you recognise a Kerry obscene telephone call?
  Heavy belching.

☺ ☺ ☺

What is the definition of an intellectual Kerryman?
  One who goes to an art gallery even when it's not raining.

☺ ☺ ☺

How do you recognise a Kerry raffle?
  Tickets are €1 each or a book of €10 for €11.

☺ ☺ ☺

Why did the Kerryman stipulate that there should be no flowers at his funeral?
  He was allergic to them.

☺ ☺ ☺

How does a Kerry doctor console a Kerry widow?
  Thank God he didn't die of anything serious.

☺ ☺ ☺

Have you heard about the Kerry crematorium?
  It caught fire and all the bodies were burned to death.

☺ ☺ ☺

Why are Kerry snow ploughs so useless?
  The drivers refuse to operate them when the weather is really bad.

☺ ☺ ☺

Have you heard about the Kerryman's dog who was sitting by the fire chewing a bone?

When he got up he realised he had only three legs.

☺ ☺ ☺

What did the Kerryman choose as his special subject on *Mastermind*?

Polish popes of the twentieth century.

☺ ☺ ☺

What is a Kerryman's favourite drink?

The next one.

☺ ☺ ☺

Why did the Kerryman eat Tampax?

Because he wanted to be able to swim, ski and even parachute at any time of the month.

☺ ☺ ☺

What is the best-selling Kerry cookbook?

365 Ways to Cook a Potato.

☺ ☺ ☺

What would a Kerryman be if he wasn't a Kerryman?

Ashamed of himself.

☺ ☺ ☺

What is the withdrawal policy of a Kerry bank?

You can draw your money out at any instant provided you give two weeks' notice.

Why was there a delay in introducing the new currency into Kerry?

They were waiting for all the old people to die.

☺   ☺   ☺

What happens to a Kerryman who doesn't pay his garbage bill?

They stop delivering.

☺   ☺   ☺

Why couldn't the Kerryman read the daily newspaper?

Because he had gone to night school.

☺   ☺   ☺

What do you call a Kerryman who knows how to control a wife?

A bachelor.

☺   ☺   ☺

When were the good old days in Kerry?

When you could go into a restaurant with €1, get a meal, a drink and a good overcoat.

☺   ☺   ☺

Have you heard about the Kerryman who invented an electric car and drove from Tralee to Dublin?

The electricity cost him only €5 but the extension cord cost him €100,000.

☺   ☺   ☺

What did the Kerryman say the first time he saw a lobster pot?
    How would you get a lobster to sit on one of those things?

☺   ☺   ☺

Why was the Kerryman's house hit by a jumbo jet?
    He left the landing light on.

☺   ☺   ☺

Have you heard about the Kerry skunk?
    He fell in love with a gas leak.

☺   ☺   ☺

Why was the Kerry forger arrested?
    He was caught with €10 million €9 notes.

☺   ☺   ☺

What is every Kerry burglar's ambition?
    To learn how to pick the locks of pay toilets.

☺   ☺   ☺

How do you recognise a Kerryman's watch?
    It can do an hour in forty-five minutes.

☺   ☺   ☺

Why was the Kerryman painting his house at a furious rate?
    He wanted to finish before the paint ran out.

☺   ☺   ☺

Why did the Kerry prisoner who tunnelled his way out of jail give himself up to the police?

He told them he was only practising for the mass breakout at the end of the month.

☺   ☺   ☺

Why was boxing never popular in Kerry?

Nobody could count.

☺   ☺   ☺

Why was the Kerryman laughing hysterically as he was to be hanged?

Because they were hanging the wrong man.

☺   ☺   ☺

What is the most popular dish in Kerry restaurants?

Soup in the basket.

☺   ☺   ☺

What did the Kerryman think when he saw a roll of sello-tape?

He thought it was glue sniffer's packed lunch.

☺   ☺   ☺

Have you heard about the Kerryman who bet that he could lean further out the window than his brother?

He won.

☺   ☺   ☺

What do you call a 300-pound Kerryman with a sawn-off shotgun?
Sir!

☺   ☺   ☺

What is the best-selling girlie magazine in Kerry?
Ploughboy.

☺   ☺   ☺

How do you make a Kerrywoman pregnant?
You don't know? And you think Kerrymen are dumb!

☺   ☺   ☺

What do you call a Kerryman with six honours in his Leaving Cert?
A liar.

☺   ☺   ☺

What did the Kerryman say when the judge offered him thirty days or €100?
I'll take the €100.

☺   ☺   ☺

What is the definition of a true Kerryman?
Someone who goes to a topless bar just to get drunk.

☺   ☺   ☺

Why do Kerry businessmen not take coffee after lunch?
It keeps them awake all afternoon.

How do you recognise a Kerry Polo mint?
    The hole is on the outside.

☺   ☺   ☺

How does a Kerry photographer manage if he hasn't got a darkroom?
    He just wears a blindfold.

☺   ☺   ☺

How much do haircuts cost in Kerry?
    €8 – €2 a corner.

☺   ☺   ☺

How do you recognise a Kerry mousetrap?
    It comes complete with its own mice.

☺   ☺   ☺

How do you recognise a formal Kerry dinner?
    When all the men come to the table with their flies zipped up.

☺   ☺   ☺

What do you call a Kerryman who carries only a sawn-off shotgun and a switchblade?
    A pacifist.

☺   ☺   ☺

Have you heard about the Kerry karate expert?
    He killed himself saluting.

How do you know if you are being mugged by a Kerryman?
  You have to show him what to do.

☺   ☺   ☺

How does a Kerryman call a cab?
  He puts his fingers in his mouth and shouts 'Taxi'.

☺   ☺   ☺

What did the Kerryman say when he went to the ballet for the first time?
  'Why don't they get taller girls?'

☺   ☺   ☺

What does a Kerry bank clerk say when you hand him money?
  'For me?'

☺   ☺   ☺

Why was the Kerryman standing in front of the mirror with his eyes closed?
  He wanted to see what he looked like when he was asleep.

☺   ☺   ☺

What did the Kerryman say when he saw a moose head on a wall?
  'He must have been going at a fair old pace when he hit that wall.'

☺   ☺   ☺

Why did the Kerryman spend two hours in a revolving door?
  He was trying to slam it.

Have you heard about the Kerryman who kept reading that cigarette smoking was bad for him?

He gave up reading.

☺   ☺   ☺

Have you heard about the Kerry girl who came second in a beauty contest?

She was the only entrant.

☺   ☺   ☺

What does a Kerryman say when he sees a man playing the trombone?

'There must be some trick to it – he can't really be swallowing it.'

☺   ☺   ☺

Why did the Kerryman buy a house next to the pawnshop?

So he could keep an eye on his property.

☺   ☺   ☺

How did the gang of robbers escape from a Kerry superstore?

The police had surrounded all of the exits so they must have escaped through an entrance.

☺   ☺   ☺

Why did the Kerryman take his pregnant wife to the supermarket?

He heard they made free deliveries.

☺   ☺   ☺

How do you recognise a Kerry car pool?
They all meet at work.

☺ ☺ ☺

Why did the Kerryman shoot his packet of cornflakes?
  He was a cereal killer.

☺ ☺ ☺

How do you recognise a Kerry intellectual?
  He can read without moving his lips.

☺ ☺ ☺

Why did the bald Kerryman refuse to have a transplant?
  He thought he'd look daft with a kidney on his head.

☺ ☺ ☺

Have you heard about the Kerryman who tried to commit suicide with an elastic rope?
  He died of concussion.

☺ ☺ ☺

How does a Kerryman do a 'Spot the Ball' entry?
  He prods around his newspaper with a pin until he hears 'psst'.

☺ ☺ ☺

Why do Kerry elephants drink?
  It helps them to forget.

☺ ☺ ☺

Have you heard about the Kerryman who joined the mafia?
They made him an offer he couldn't understand.

☺   ☺   ☺

How do you recognise a really classy Kerryman?
All the words on his tattoo are spelled correctly.

☺   ☺   ☺

What did the Kerryman do when his pet canary lost its sight in an accident?
He took it to the Bird's Eye factory.

☺   ☺   ☺

Why did the Kerryman quit his job as a taxi-driver?
He couldn't stand people talking behind his back.

☺   ☺   ☺

How do you confuse a Kerryman?
Put him in a barrel and tell him to stand in a corner.

☺   ☺   ☺

What did the Kerryman do when he heard that 90% of car accidents happen within five miles of home?
He moved house.

☺   ☺   ☺

How do you recognise a posh Kerry household?
They have grapes even when nobody is sick.

☺   ☺   ☺

Why did the Kerryman quit his job as a fireman?

It used to take him nearly two hours to climb back up the pole.

☺ ☺ ☺

Why do Kerrymen carry umbrellas when it's not raining?

Because umbrellas can't walk!

☺ ☺ ☺

What do you get if you cross a Kerryman with an elephant?

A Kerryman who will never forget you, a dirty look from the elephant, and the Nobel prize for biology.

☺ ☺ ☺

Why do Kerrymen wear bowler hats?

To protect their heads from woodpeckers.

☺ ☺ ☺

Have you heard about the Kerryman who does wonderful work for hospitals?

He makes people sick.

☺ ☺ ☺

Have you heard about the Kerryman who died in China?

They buried him in a paddy-field!

☺ ☺ ☺

Have you heard about the Kerryman who lost €10 on the Grand National?

Worse still, he lost €20 on the television re-run.

Have you heard about the Kerry seaside village that was reputed to be the dullest place in the world?

One day the tide went out and never came back in again.

☺ ☺ ☺

How do you sink a Kerry submarine?

Knock on the door.

☺ ☺ ☺

What does a Kerryman say while making an obscene telephone call?

'Stop telling me the time while I'm talking to you.'

☺ ☺ ☺

What happened when Kerry grave-diggers went on strike?

There was a wave of panic dying.

☺ ☺ ☺

Why do Kerrymen never take their wives out?

Their mothers warn them not to go out with married women.

☺ ☺ ☺

How do you recognise the instruction manual for a Kerry car?

Easy – it's a bus timetable.

☺ ☺ ☺

What do you call a Kerryman with his ears stuffed with cotton wool?

Anything you like – he can't hear you.

How does the system of yellow lines on Kerry streets operate?
    One yellow line means no parking at all. Two yellow lines means no parking at all at all.

☺ ☺ ☺

What do you call a Kerryman in a suit?
    The defendant.

☺ ☺ ☺

Have you heard about the Kerry chess champion?
    He played blindfolded against twelve Soviet grandmasters simultaneously and was annihilated in all twelve matches.

☺ ☺ ☺

Why did the Kerryman spend three hours in a carwash?
    He thought it was raining too hard to drive.

☺ ☺ ☺

Why does a Kerryman's car have heated rear windows?
    To keep his hands warm while he is pushing it.

☺ ☺ ☺

How do you recognise a Kerryman's pencil?
    It's got an eraser at both ends.

☺ ☺ ☺

How do you recognise a Kerryman's word processor?
    The screen is covered in Tippex.

☺ ☺ ☺

What does a Kerry blacksmith say to his assistant?

'I'll put the red-hot iron on the anvil and, when I nod my head, you hit it.'

☺ ☺ ☺

Have you heard about the Kerry acid bath murderer?

He lost an arm taking the stopper out of the plughole.

☺ ☺ ☺

Why did the Kerryman lose his job as a lift operator?

He couldn't remember his route.

☺ ☺ ☺

Why was the Kerryman jumping up and down on a hedge-hog?

He wanted a really big conker.

☺ ☺ ☺

How did the Kerryman injure himself at a Halloween party?

He was bobbing for chips.

☺ ☺ ☺

Have you heard about the Kerry burglar who went to America?

He was caught stealing the lead off the roof of Fort Knox.

☺ ☺ ☺

How do you double the value of a Kerryman's car?

Fill the tank with petrol.

How do you recognise a Kerryman's crystal tableware?

Two empty jars of the same brand of peanut butter.

☺   ☺   ☺

How long does it take a Kerryman to write a note to the milkman?

About an hour – even longer if he forgets to write on the paper before he puts it into the bottle.

☺   ☺   ☺

What is the best time to sell land to a Kerryman?

When the tide is out.

☺   ☺   ☺

Have you heard about the Kerryman who tunnelled his way to freedom from prison in two months?

He was serving only one month.

☺   ☺   ☺

Have you heard about the Kerryman who committed suicide by drinking a can of varnish?

He had a terrible end but a beautiful finish.

☺   ☺   ☺

How many Kerrymen does it take to make popcorn?

Ten – one to hold the pan and nine to shake the cooker up and down.

☺   ☺   ☺

What happened to the Kerry cannibal who went on a self-catering holiday?

He came back with two wooden legs.

☺   ☺   ☺

A Kerryman went to confession and when he had confessed his sins he was told by the priest to say the Our Father for his penance.

'I'm afraid I don't know that prayer,' said the Kerryman.

'How about the Hail Mary?' said the priest.

'I don't know that either,' said the Kerryman.

'Is there any prayer you do know?' asked the priest.

'Yes,' said the Kerryman, 'there's the Angelus.'

'Well, you can say that if you like,' said the priest.

'Bong, Bong, Bong,' said the Kerryman.

☺   ☺   ☺

A Kerryman was told that if he could answer one general knowledge question he would be given a job as a road sweeper.

'What does Aurora Borealis mean?' asked the interviewer.

'It means I don't get the job,' said the Kerryman.

☺   ☺   ☺

Two Kerrymen went up to Dublin for the All-Ireland football final and went out drinking on Friday night. When they woke up on Saturday afternoon, they thought it was Sunday, so they hired a taxi to take them to the big match. The taxi driver took them to Landsdowne Road where a big rugby match was in progress. After a while one Kerryman said, 'It's a very rough match, isn't it?'

'Yes,' said the other, 'and it must have been a heck of a minor match too. Look at the shape of the ball after it.'

☺   ☺   ☺

Have you heard about the Kerry Jew?
　He translated the Bible into Hebrew.

☺　☺　☺

Have you heard about the Kerryman who walked into a record store and asked for the latest single by Marcel Marceau?

☺　☺　☺

Kerryman giving directions to a tourist:
'Drive down the road about two miles until you come to a small whitewashed cottage. Ignore that completely. Then proceed for another bit and turn left where the old milestone used to be. Stick to the tar and you can't miss it.'

☺　☺　☺

It is now thought that the word 'bungalow' was invented by two Kerry builders. They were building a two-storey house when they ran out of building blocks. 'I'll tell you what,' said one to the other, 'we'll bung a low roof on it and leave it at that.'

☺　☺　☺

An old Kerrywoman was explaining to her neighbours that she didn't like teabags.
　'By the time you'd have the corners cut off them and the tea taken out of them you'd have been as well off buying a full half-pound of tea in a packet in the first place.'

☺　☺　☺

Two Kerrymen were sent to jail in a high security prison but they developed an ingenious method of communicating with each other by means of a secret code and banging on the pipes.

However, their scheme broke down when they were transferred to different cells.

☺ ☺ ☺

An American tourist was being shown around Kerry by a local guide.

'Say Mac,' said the American, 'what's that mountain over there?'

'That's Carrantouhill,' said the Kerryman, 'it's the highest mountain in the world.'

'But what about Mount Everest?' said the American.

'Oh exceptin' those in foreign parts,' said the Kerryman.

☺ ☺ ☺

A Kerryman was asked if he would buy a nuclear fall-out shelter in case of a nuclear attack.

'They're a bit expensive,' he replied, 'I think I'll wait and see if I can pick up a good cheap second-hand one.'

☺ ☺ ☺

Customer in Kerry restaurant: 'I'll have asparagus.'
Kerry waiter: 'We don't serve sparrows, but how did you know my name was Gus?'

☺ ☺ ☺

The Annual General Meeting of the Kerry Claustrophobia Society has just been held. Only one member turned up at the hall and he kept shouting, 'let me out, let me out.'

A tourist in Kerry noticed that the two clocks on the church tower showed different times, so he asked a Kerryman to explain.

'Look,' said the Kerryman, 'if both clocks showed the same time, we would need only one clock.'

☺   ☺   ☺

Have you heard about the Kerry footballer who scored a goal in the All-Ireland final?

He missed it on the action replay.

☺   ☺   ☺

Notice in a Kerry pub:
'The management will not be responsible for any injuries incurred in the mad rush for the door at closing time.'

☺   ☺   ☺

A Kerryman took a body-building course from Charles Atlas. After it was over, he wrote the following letter:

'Dear Sir,

I have now finished the course, so please send on the muscles.'

☺   ☺   ☺

A Kerryman was in court charged with stealing a cow.

'How do you plead?' asked the judge.

'Not guilty,' said the Kerryman.

'Is this the first time you've been up before me?' asked the judge.

'I don't know,' said the Kerryman, 'what time do you get up at?'

'No,' said the judge, 'I mean is this the first time you've been in court?'

'Yes,' said the Kerryman, 'I've never stolen anything before.'

The court erupted with laughter so the judge shouted 'order, order.'

'I'll have a pint,' said the Kerryman.

☺   ☺   ☺

It was the Kerry chess championships and two Kerry grandmasters were sitting with their heads bent over the board, contemplating their strategies. Radio, television and the newspapers waited with bated breath for the next move. Hours went by and there was no sign of anything happening. The one of the Kerry grandmasters looked up and said, 'Oh! Is it my move?'

☺   ☺   ☺

'Can you play the violin?' a Kerryman was asked in an interview.

'I don't know,' he replied, 'I've never tried.'

☺   ☺   ☺

A French lady settled in Kerry so the local coal merchant decided to call on her to see if she required any coal.

'How do you deliver your coal?' she asked him.

'You have a choice,' said the Kerryman, 'you can have it coal-de-sack or a la cart.'

☺   ☺   ☺

First Kerry businessman: 'How is business?'
Second Kerry businessman: 'Terrible, it's the worst year I can ever remember. Even the people who never pay me haven't bought anything this year.'

A Kerryman and his wife were going on a picnic so they drove out into the countryside, parked their car and walked a few miles in the woods.

'I hope you've remembered to put the car keys in a safe place,' said the Kerrywoman.

'Of course,' said the Kerryman, 'I've locked them in the boot.'

☺   ☺   ☺

A tourist travelling in Kerry saw a very dangerous unprotected cliff with no warning notice on it, so he asked a Kerryman why this was the case.

'Well,' said the Kerryman, 'we did have a warning notice, but nobody ever fell over the cliff, so we took the notice away.'

☺   ☺   ☺

A Kerry economist has just come up with a fantastic new plan to shorten the dole queue.

He suggests that the unemployed should be lined up four abreast.

☺   ☺   ☺

'A thermos flask is a wonderful invention,' said a Kerryman, 'but there's one thing about it I cannot understand. If you put hot tea in the flask, it keeps it hot, but if you put chilled orange juice in it, it keeps it cold; how does it know?'

☺   ☺   ☺

A Kerryman was on trial for stealing a car. He explained that it was parked outside a cemetery and that he had taken it because he thought the owner was dead.

A Kerryman was told by his bank manager that his current account was €500 overdrawn and that he would have to balance it at once.

'I'm terribly sorry about that,' said the Kerryman, 'and I'll see to it immediately. Can I give you a cheque?'

☺ ☺ ☺

Have you heard about the Kerryman who applied for an unlisted telephone number because he didn't have a telephone?

☺ ☺ ☺

A Kerryman's explanation of the yellow lines on the roads:

One yellow line means you have to park with two wheels on the pavement. Two yellow lines means you have to park with all four wheels on the pavement.

☺ ☺ ☺

A Kerry jarvey was driving a tourist around the Lakes of Killarney.

'Look,' said the tourist, 'that's the thinnest horse I've ever seen in my life – why don't you fatten him up a bit?'

'Fatten him up, is it?' said the Kerryman, 'the poor beast can hardly carry all the meat that's on him now.'

☺ ☺ ☺

A Kerryman was sentenced to a total of 500 years in prison for a series of crimes he had committed. He appealed and got his sentence reduced to 400 years.

☺ ☺ ☺

A Kerry explorer was heading for the North Pole with his faithful dog Rover. However, he ran out of food and was forced to eat the poor old dog. As he licked the bones clean, he said, 'poor old Rover would have loved those bones.'

☺   ☺   ☺

A Kerrywoman was addressing the Annual General Meeting of the Widows' Association and she told her listeners:

'I'm very glad to announce a large increase in membership since last year.'

☺   ☺   ☺

Two Kerrymen escaped from jail and were being followed by the police with tracker dogs. The two Kerrymen decided to climb up into the trees in order to escape. As the dogs came sniffing at the base of the tree where the first Kerryman was hiding he went, 'meow, meow'.

'Come away,' said the policeman, 'that's only a cat.'

The dogs then began to sniff at the base of the tree where the second Kerryman was hiding.

'Moo, moo,' went the second Kerryman.

☺   ☺   ☺

Kerry boxer (during a break in a fight): 'How am I doing, coach?'

Coach: 'Let me put it this way – you'll have to knock him out now to get a draw.'

☺   ☺   ☺

A Kerryman was one of the world's most famous clairvoyants. He even knew beforehand the day he would die because the judge told him.

The EU road fund has just given €100 million to improve the Kerry bypass.

It's going to be used to repair the Cork–Limerick road.

☺   ☺   ☺

Sign seen in Kerry:
'Metrication office – 100 yards.'

☺   ☺   ☺

A Kerryman and his wife had a pretty rough marriage – they had four endorsements on their marriage licence.

☺   ☺   ☺

A Kerryman called round to see his doctor.

'How are you?' asked the doctor, 'I haven't seen you for ages.'

'That's right,' said the Kerryman, 'I haven't been very well.'

☺   ☺   ☺

A Kerryman at the theatre was looking for the gentlemen's toilet so he asked the doorman where it was.

'Go down the corridor,' said the doorman, 'turn left and the urinal is there on your right.'

'Actually,' said the Kerryman, 'what I really want is the arsenal.'

☺   ☺   ☺

A Kerryman was seen leaving the theatre at the interval during a new play.

'Excuse me sir,' said the doorman, 'isn't the play to your liking?'

'It's not that at all,' said the Kerryman, 'it's just that the programme says that the second act takes place two weeks later and my mother told me to be home before midnight.'

☺   ☺   ☺

A Kerry teenage girl went to her father and asked him if she could have some money to go and see *Grease*.

He bought her a return ticket to Athens.

☺   ☺   ☺

Two Kerrymen, one very fat and the other very thin, once decided to fight a duel with pistols. Their seconds decided that the thin man had an unfair advantage because of the bigger target that the fat man presented. Finally they agreed that the figure of the thin man be chalked on the body of the fat man and that any bullets hitting the fat man outside the line would not count.

☺   ☺   ☺

A Kerryman opened an antique shop and one day an American tourist came in and offered him €10 for an antique vase.

'Take it, though it cost me €20 to buy.'

'But how on earth do you manage to stay in business at that rate?' asked the astonished American.

'Sssh,' said the Kerryman, 'I just make a wrong entry in the ledger.'

☺   ☺   ☺

Have you heard about the Kerry string quartet?

It would have been a sextet only two of them were refused bail.

Four Kerrymen were playing poker while a Corkman looked on. At one stage the Corkman spotted the dealer giving himself four aces from the bottom of the deck. When he drew the attention of the other three Kerrymen to what had happened, one of them said casually, 'what of it, wasn't it his deal?'

☺　☺　☺

A landlord had a Kerryman staying in one of his flats so to make sure that the heating was maintained at the correct temperature he supplied the Kerryman with a thermometer.

'Do you know how to use it?' he asked him.

'Yes,' said the Kerryman, 'I sit and watch it until it rises over the critical temperature and then I take it into the garden to cool.'

☺　☺　☺

Have you heard about the Kerry typist who thought that punctuation meant being at the office on time every morning?

☺　☺　☺

An old Kerryman was due to go into hospital for an operation for many years, so he finally plucked up the courage. As soon as he arrived at the hospital he was given a thorough bath.

'Well,' he said to himself, 'thank goodness that's over, I've been dreading that operation for years.'

☺　☺　☺

A society lady went to a famous Kerry artist and asked him if he would paint a portrait of her in the nude for €1,000.

'Certainly,' said the Kerryman, 'but can I leave my socks on because I must have somewhere to put my brushes.'

Have you heard about the Kerry cow who went out for a night and drank more than was good for her?

She woke up with a terrible hangunder.

☺   ☺   ☺

Newspaper report of a Kerry funeral: 'At the graveside the son-in-law of the deceased collapsed and died. Naturally this threw a gloom over the entire proceedings.'

☺   ☺   ☺

Here is a sad little story about a Kerryman with two wooden legs – Fire broke out in his house and he was burned to the ground. He tried to claim money from the insurance company, but he was told he didn't have a leg to stand on. In fact he was accused of arson and being a low down bum.

☺   ☺   ☺

A Kerryman emigrated to America and one of the first sights he saw was a dead millionaire being buried. The millionaire was dressed in a mohair suit and was encased in a golden coffin studded with diamonds.

'Now that,' said the Kerryman, 'is what I call really living.'

☺   ☺   ☺

A newly rich Kerryman stayed the night in a big Dublin hotel. Next morning the porter asked him if he had slept well.

'Not really,' said the Kerryman, 'I was afraid that somebody would want to take a bath and the only way to the bathroom was through my bedroom.'

☺   ☺   ☺

Have you heard about the Kerryman who thought that a knighthood was a cap for keeping his ears warm when he was asleep.

☺ ☺ ☺

A doctor was treating a Kerrywoman for her nerves and having given her a complete examination informed her that she had acute paranoia.
'Look doctor,' she told him, 'I've come here to be treated, not to be admired.'

☺ ☺ ☺

Newsflash!!
Thieves escaped with over half a million euro from a Kerry bank last night.

Police are baffled trying to figure out the motive for the crime.

☺ ☺ ☺

A Kerryman claimed that he had a talking dog who was a genius at mathematics. He used to ask him what five, minus three, minus two was, and the dog used to say nothing.

☺ ☺ ☺

A Kerryman and his wife were on their honeymoon in a big hotel. About one o'clock the Kerryman's wife awoke and said she was thirsty so he went down the corridor and got her a drink of water. About two o'clock she awoke again so the Kerryman got her another drink. Finally, she awoke at three o'clock and again said she was thirsty, so once again the Kerryman set off down the corridor. About half an hour later he returned with a glass of water.

'What kept you so long?' she asked him.

'Sorry for the delay,' said the Kerryman, 'but there was a fellow sitting on the well.'

☺   ☺   ☺

A Kerryman went into a bar, ordered a bottle of whiskey and proceeded to drink every drop of it. Then, he got up and started to leave.

'Hey,' said the bartender, 'how about paying for the whiskey?'

'Look,' said the Kerryman, 'did you pay for it?'

'Of course I did,' said the barman.

'Well there's no point in both of us paying for it, is there?' said the Kerryman, and walked out.

☺   ☺   ☺

Have you heard about the Kerrywoman who was asked what she would do if her hot pants went on fire?

She said she would put out the blaze with her panty hose.

☺   ☺   ☺

A Kerryman buying a pair of shoes was asked by the sales assistant what size shoes he took.

'I take size eights,' said the Kerryman, 'but I always find they're a bit tight for me, so I think I'll try on a pair of size nines for a start.'

☺   ☺   ☺

'Is this soldier dangerously wounded?' a Kerry doctor was asked.

'Two of the wounds are fatal,' he replied, 'but the third can be cured, provided the patient gets a few weeks rest.'

Two Kerrymen were sitting by the seashore watching the dredger at work in the harbour.

'Let's go home,' said one Kerryman, 'I've seen enough.'

'No,' said the second, 'I'm not going until I've seen the last of those buckets coming up out of the water. There's been over a thousand of them so far so there couldn't be many left.'

☺ ☺ ☺

Tourist in Kerry restaurant: 'I ordered French sardines. Are you sure these sardines you just served me are French?'
Kerry waiter: 'I couldn't say sir, they were past speaking when we opened the tin.'

☺ ☺ ☺

'There's one thing we must admire the Chinese for,' exclaimed a Kerryman, 'and that's for learning to speak their own language.'

☺ ☺ ☺

Kerry doctor: 'Have you taken that box of pills I prescribed for you?'
Kerry patient: 'I took the whole box, but I don't feel a bit better yet.'
Kerry doctor: 'Just wait until the lid comes off.'

☺ ☺ ☺

'Has anybody ever been lost in this lake?' a tourist once asked a Kerry boatman.

'No,' said the Kerryman, 'nobody has ever been lost here. My brother was drowned here last month but they found him two days later.'

☺ ☺ ☺

Two very sick Kerrymen were on the boat to England. One said to the other: 'Mick, for God's sake ask the captain to stop the ship for a minutes until I get a rest, or I'll have to get out and walk.'

☺   ☺   ☺

'I was that strong when I was a child,' boasted a Kerryman, 'that I could lift up my own pram with myself inside it.'

☺   ☺   ☺

A Kerrywoman boasted that her husband was a great animal lover. She claimed he once put his shirt on a bleedin' horse that was scratched.

☺   ☺   ☺

One Kerryman was telling another about his travels and adventures in Africa. 'I once saw a man with his hands tied behind his back being beheaded,' he told him, 'and do you know what happened – he picked up his head and put it back on his shoulders again.'

'How could he do that?' asked the second Kerryman, 'when his hands were tied behind his back?'

'You fool,' said the first Kerryman, 'couldn't he pick it up with his teeth?'

☺   ☺   ☺

A Kerryman received his army conscription papers so he wrote back saying that he couldn't join because he had a wooden leg. A second letter arrived asking him to give further details of how he came to have a wooden leg. He replied as follows:

'My father had a wooden leg and so had his father before him. It runs in the family.'

Kerry foreman: 'Where did you put that sledge hammer I gave you?'

Kerry workman: 'I can't find it – I must have lost it.'

Kerry foreman: 'I'll break every bone in your body with it if you don't find it.'

☺   ☺   ☺

Two Kerrymen were working on a building site when one of them fell a hundred feet to the ground. The other Kerryman rushed to his side and shouted, 'Mick, are you killed? If you're dead speak to me.'

Mick opened one eye and said, 'no, Tim, I'm not dead, I'm merely knocked speechless.'

☺   ☺   ☺

A Kerryman went to confession and told the priest that he had stolen some turf.

'How much turf did you steal?' asked the priest.

'I may as well confess to stealing a full stack, because I'm going back for the rest of it tonight.'

☺   ☺   ☺

A Kerryman and his wife had trouble in planning their family so their local parish priest advised them to use the rhythm method.

'It's all very well for him to talk,' said the Kerryman, 'but where am I going to get a ceilí band at one o'clock in the morning.'

☺   ☺   ☺

It was two Kerrymen who kidnapped the body of Charlie Chaplin.

They threatened to shoot him if they weren't paid €1 million ransom.

☺   ☺   ☺

A Kerryman went to a dance but wasn't having much success with the girls so he asked his friend for advice.

'Whisper something romantic in her ear,' said the friend, 'girls seem to like that sort of thing.'

A few minutes later the Kerryman returned with a black eye.

'What on earth is the matter,' asked the friend, 'did you whisper something romantic in her ear?'

'I did,' said the Kerryman.

'And what did you whisper?' asked the friend.

'Well,' said the Kerryman, 'I whispered the most romantic thing I could think of; I told her she didn't sweat much for a fat girl.'

☺   ☺   ☺

A Kerryman was asked if he would join a nudist colony. He refused saying that if nature had intended him to be a nudist, he would have been born without any clothes on.

☺   ☺   ☺

Two Kerrymen went into a café to have a cup of tea. They were given a sugar bowl with sugar lumps.

'Hold on,' said the first Kerryman, 'I haven't been given a teaspoon.'

'That's all right, I've got two,' said the second Kerryman breaking the sugar tongs.

☺   ☺   ☺

Have you heard about the Kerryman who had one arm shorter than the other.

He got a job as a shorthand typist.

☺   ☺   ☺

A big game hunter was showing a Kerryman the heads of all the animals he had shot, mounted on his living-room wall.

'If we go into the other room,' asked the Kerryman, 'can we see the other end of the animals?'

☺   ☺   ☺

First Kerryman: 'My uncle died during a tightrope performance.'
Second Kerryman: 'I didn't know he worked in a circus.'
First Kerryman: 'He didn't – he was hanged.'

☺   ☺   ☺

A Kerryman was being interviewed for a life insurance policy.

'Have you ever had an accident?' asked the clerk.

'No,' said the Kerryman, 'but once I was kicked by a horse and trampled on.'

'Don't you consider those accidents?' asked the clerk.

'No,' said the Kerryman, 'he did it on purpose.'

☺   ☺   ☺

Have you heard about the Kerry lifeguard?

He was trying to give a fellow he had rescued artificial respiration, but the fellow kept getting up and walking away.

☺   ☺   ☺

A Kerry worm was crawling up out of the ground when he saw the most beautiful worm he had ever seen crawling up out of the ground near him.

'Say baby,' he said, 'how about you and me getting together?'

'We already are,' came the reply, 'I'm your other end.'

☺   ☺   ☺

What does a Kerryman use for a pocket calculator?

A rabbit – because he heard that rabbits multiply rapidly.

☺   ☺   ☺

A tourist holidaying in Kerry was astonished to find a pub open and filled with drinkers at two o'clock in the morning.

'Say,' he said to the barman, 'when do the pubs shut around here?'

'About the middle of October,' said the barman.

☺   ☺   ☺

A tourist was being driven around Kerry by a local jarvey when he saw a fine house up on a hill.

'Who lives there?' he asked.

'The late widow O'Keeffe,' said the jarvey.

'When did she die?' asked the tourist.

'If she had lived until next Tuesday,' said the jarvey, 'she would have been dead a year.'

☺   ☺   ☺

Have you heard about the Kerryman who went to a Freemason and asked him if he would build him a house for nothing?

☺   ☺   ☺

Have you heard about the Kerryman who went on a sea voyage and complained because he wasn't invited to dine at the captain's table?

He was told that dining at the captain's table wasn't the usual custom on the Killimer car ferry.

☺   ☺   ☺

A Kerryman applied for a credit card and the manager of the credit card company asked if he had much money in the bank.

'I have,' said the Kerryman.

'How much?' asked the manager.

'I don't know exactly,' said the Kerryman, 'I haven't shaken it lately.'

☺   ☺   ☺

Have you heard about the Kerry glassblower who inhaled instead of exhaling?

He got a pane in the stomach.

☺   ☺   ☺

A Kerryman went into a big store and asked if he could buy a thermometer.

'Certainly sir,' said the clerk, 'would you like a Centigrade or a Fahrenheit one?'

'Which is the better brand?' asked the Kerryman.

☺   ☺   ☺

A Kerryman travelling by train told the ticket inspector that he wanted to get off at a certain village.

'I'm afraid we don't stop here sir,' said the inspector.

'Could you stop long enough for me to let my wife know that I'm being carried through?' asked the Kerryman.

A Kerryman called at a garage and asked if he could buy a new dip-stick for his car.

'What's the matter with the old one?' asked the attendant.

'It's too short,' said the Kerryman, 'It won't reach down to the oil.'

☺   ☺   ☺

A Kerryman went into an old-fashioned grocery store with a big jar and asked the grocer to fill it up with treacle.

The grocer did so and said, 'There you are sir, now where is your money?'

'I left it at the bottom of the jar,' said the Kerryman.

☺   ☺   ☺

A Kerryman opposed the abolition of capital punishment because if it were abolished it would be unfair to all those who had been executed over the years.

☺   ☺   ☺

A Kerryman working in an office was given custody of the only key of the mailbox. However, he went on holidays and took the key with him, so the manager phoned him up and told him the position.

The Kerryman then returned the key immediately by post.

☺   ☺   ☺

A Kerryman joined the police force and after a few months he was summoned before the district inspector.

'I'm putting you on night patrol next week,' said the inspector, 'I hope you're prepared for it.'

'Certainly,' said the Kerryman, 'my mother is going to come with me until I get used to it.'

Two Kerrymen were on holiday in Majorca, stretched out on the beach soaking in the sun.

'Hey,' said one to the other, 'isn't today the day they're playing the county football final back home in Kerry?'

'Yes,' said the other Kerryman, 'and they have a nice day for it too.'

☺   ☺   ☺

Two Kerrymen were out hunting when one of them saw a rabbit.

'Quick,' said the first Kerryman, 'shoot it.'

'I can't,' said the second, 'my gun isn't loaded.'

'Well,' said the first Kerryman, 'you know that, and I know that, but the rabbit doesn't know.'

☺   ☺   ☺

A Kerryman was hitchhiking when he was picked up by a fellow driving a Mercedes.

'What's that on the front of the car?' asked the Kerryman, pointing to the three-pronged Mercedes emblem surrounded by a circle.

'That's the sights of my front gun,' said the fellow who was a bit of a joker, 'I use it to shoot cyclists.'

'There's one in front of us now,' said the Kerryman. 'Show me how it works.'

As they passed by, the driver made some convincing shot-like noises and said 'I'm afraid we missed him.'

'No, we didn't,' said the Kerryman, 'I got him with the door of the car as we went by.'

☺   ☺   ☺

The Irish skating championships were reaching a climax when the final competitor had a bit of a mishap. He slipped just as he was entering the rink, slid across the floor on his rear end, and demolished the judges' table with his feet.

'Could I have your marks please, just for the record,' said the chief official.

'0.0,' said the Dublin judge;

'0.0,' said the Galway judge;

'0.0,' said the Cork judge;

'9.9,' said the Kerry judge;

'Hold on a moment,' said the chief official to the Kerry judge, 'how can you award such a high score for such a terrible performance?'

'Well, said the Kerry judge, 'you've got to make allowances – it's slippery as hell out there.'

☺   ☺   ☺

Policeman: 'Come out of that river, there's no bathing allowed.'
Kerryman: 'The laugh's on you, I'm not bathing, I'm drowning.'

☺   ☺   ☺

A Kerryman and his wife were staying in a hotel overnight. In the morning she asked him if he had heard all the thunder during the night.

'No,' said the Kerryman, 'I didn't hear a thing; tell me, was it loud?'

'It was the loudest I ever heard,' said the Kerrywoman, 'I thought the hotel would fall over our heads.'

'Why didn't you wake me up?' said the Kerryman, 'you know I can't sleep when there's thunder.'

☺   ☺   ☺

Have you heard about the Kerryman who entered in a slow bicycle race?

He came first.

Oil was discovered off the coast of Kerry but during operations one of the oil wells caught fire and went out of control. So they sent for Red Adair, the fire fighter, who flew in by private jet and soon blew the fire out.

Afterwards a Kerryman said to him, 'That was terrific, tell me, do you see anything of Ginger Rodgers at all these days?'

☺   ☺   ☺

A Kerryman went into a post office and asked if there were any letters for him.

'I'll see sir,' said the clerk, 'what is your name?'

'You're having me on now because I'm a Kerryman,' said the Kerryman, 'won't you see the name on the envelope.'

☺   ☺   ☺

A Kerryman's wife was about to have a baby so he rang the maternity hospital.

'Don't panic,' said the nurse over the phone, 'we will look after everything. Tell me is this her first baby?'

'No,' said the Kerryman, 'this is her husband.'

☺   ☺   ☺

On a summer's day a Kerryman dressed in two heavy overcoats was perspiring heavily as he painted his house.

'Why are you dressed like that?' asked a friend.

'The instructions on the can,' said the Kerryman, 'said to put on at least two coats.'

☺   ☺   ☺

A Kerryman went ice skating on a frozen lake but was warned that the ice was very thin.

'Not to worry,' he said, 'I'll skate on one foot.'

A fellow hired a Kerryman as his gardener and asked him how to tell young seedlings from weeds.

'Well,' said the Kerryman, 'the only sure way is to pull them all out and if they come up again they're weeds.'

☺   ☺   ☺

A Kerryman carrying a newspaper walked into a pub and asked the barman if he could tell him what date it was.

'I'm not quite sure,' said the barman, 'but why don't you look at your newspaper?'

'It's no good,' said the Kerryman, 'it's yesterday's.'

☺   ☺   ☺

Circus owner: 'You left the door of the lion's cage open all night last night.'
Kerryman: 'What matter, sure nobody in his senses would bother stealing a lion.'

☺   ☺   ☺

Lecturer: 'Here is a list of statistics about Kerry farmers broken down by age and sex.'
Voice from the back: 'What about the drink?'

☺   ☺   ☺

A Kerryman was living in digs with a number of practical jokers. One night, when he was asleep, they shaved off his fine head of hair and left him as bald as an egg. Rushing out to work in the morning, he happened to glance in the mirror.

'Crikey,' said the Kerryman, 'the landlady has called the wrong man.'

☺   ☺   ☺

Have you heard about the Kerry scientist who claimed to be cleverer than Einstein?

Well, only four men are supposed to have been able to understand Einstein's Theory of Relativity, but nobody could understand the Kerryman's theory.

☺   ☺   ☺

A Kerryman in a psychiatrist's waiting-room was running around, first bouncing his head off one wall and then off another. Then he tried to put his head into the pocket of a little man sitting in the corner.

'What's the matter with you?' said the little man.

'I'm a billiard ball,' said the Kerryman.

'Good heavens,' said the little man, 'come to the head of the queue immediately.'

☺   ☺   ☺

Two Kerrymen played a game of snooker but didn't pot a single ball all night.

'Next time,' said one of them, 'how about taking that wooden triangle from around the balls?'

☺   ☺   ☺

A Kerry lad on the run from the Black and Tans was having a quick cup of tea in the back kitchen of his parents' house, when word came that the soldiers were on his trail. Quick as a flash he bolted out the back door and ran up the mountain side like a hare. The sergeant shouted to the lad's father who was digging in the back garden.

'Stop that man at once and bring him back.'

The Kerryman shouted up the mountain after his son: 'Come back here Danjoe, and let the gentleman shoot you.'

A Kerryman used to take six lumps of sugar in his tea. However, he never stirred it because he didn't like it too sweet.

☺ ☺ ☺

A Kerryman was taking his driving test and to the examiner's amazement he went straight through a red light.

'Why did you do that?' he asked the Kerryman, 'we might have been killed.'

'Not to worry,' grinned the Kerryman, 'the brother, who's an expert driver, told me to drive through the red – he's been doing it for years and he's never had an accident.'

A couple of minutes later the Kerryman drove straight through another red light.

'Look,' screamed the examiner, 'you really are trying to kill me.'

Then they came to a green light and the Kerryman slammed on his brakes nearly sending the examiner through the windscreen.

'What the heck did you do that for?' he roared.

'I always stop when the lights are green,' explained the Kerryman, 'after all the brother might be coming the other way.'

☺ ☺ ☺

How do you recognise a Kerry striptease artiste?

She's got a sugan for a g-string.

☺ ☺ ☺

A Kerryman had bought his first mirror and was using it while shaving. The mirror fell on the floor but fortunately was undamaged. As he gazed down at his face in the mirror he reflected: 'Just my luck. I've only just bought a new mirror and I've gone and cut my head off.'

A hotel manager noticed that one of his guests had signed himself XX in the register. He called round to the guest's room and found himself face to face with a Kerryman who explained, 'The first X stands for John O'Sullivan and the second X stands for M.A.'

☺   ☺   ☺

A Kerryman attended a concert where a ventriloquist who fancied himself as a comedian told about twenty Kerryman jokes in a row.

'Look,' shouted the Kerryman, standing up in the audience, 'I'm fed up being insulted by all these jokes. We're not as stupid as you make out.'

'Please sit down sir and be calm,' said the ventriloquist, 'after all it's only a joke, and don't tell me that Kerrymen haven't got a sense of humour.'

'I'm not talking to you,' said the Kerryman, 'I'm talking to the little fellow on your knee.'

☺   ☺   ☺

Two Kerrymen were sent to jail, one for thirty years and the other for thirty-five years. They happened to share the same cell, so on their first night in jail the Kerryman who got the longer sentence said to his cellmate, 'You take the bed nearest the door, since you'll be released first.'

☺   ☺   ☺

A Kerryman rang Aer Lingus and asked how long it took to fly from Dublin to London.

'Just a minute sir,' said the girl on the desk.

'Thank you,' said the Kerryman and hung up.

☺   ☺   ☺

Kerry foreman on a building site: 'How many men are working in that pit?'
Voice from pit: 'Three.'
Kerry foreman: 'Well, half of ye come up.'

☺   ☺   ☺

A Kerryman got a job reading gas meters and after his first day's work arrived up at the pub with his pockets bulging with coins and ordered drinks for everybody.

'You seem to be in the money,' said the barman; 'I suppose it will be drinks all round again when you get paid at the weekend.'

'What,' said the Kerryman, 'do I get paid as well?'

☺   ☺   ☺

Have you ever seen a Kerryman's alarm clock?

It has a long piece of string attached. All he has got to do is pull the string five minutes before the time the clock is set for, and it wakes him.

☺   ☺   ☺

Two Kerrymen emigrated to America, and were sitting in New York harbour thinking of home. A diver suddenly emerged from the water near where they sat.

'Will you look at that,' said one Kerryman to the other, 'why didn't we save the boat fare by walking to America?'

☺   ☺   ☺

A Kerryman won a round-the-world cruise in a raffle. He refused to accept his prize because he said that he had no way of getting back.

A Corkman was brought to court for pushing a Kerryman off the top of Cork's County Hall – the tallest building in Ireland.

'You shouldn't have done that you know,' said the judge, 'you might have hurt somebody walking below.'

☺   ☺   ☺

A Kerrywoman met the doctor who was treating her husband. 'Did you take his temperature this morning as I told you?' he asked.

'Indeed I did, doctor,' she replied, 'I took the barometer from the hall and put it on his chest. It said "very dry", so I gave him two bottles of stout and he recovered immediately.'

☺   ☺   ☺

A Kerry guard was giving evidence at a court case arising out of a motor accident.

'I measured the distance between the skid marks and the footpath,' he said, 'and found that it was exactly the same as the distance between the footpath and the skid marks.'

☺   ☺   ☺

How do you confuse a Kerryman?
Place three shovels against the wall and tell him to take his pick.

☺   ☺   ☺

A Kerryman charged with murder was sent for trial by jury.

To everyone's surprise he pleaded guilty. Nevertheless the jury returned a verdict of 'not guilty'.

'How on earth have you reached a verdict like that?' asked the judge, 'the man pleaded guilty.'

'You don't know him like we do, your honour,' said the foreman of the jury. 'He's the biggest liar in the country and you can't believe a word out of his mouth.'

☺   ☺   ☺

A fellow was charged with murder, so he bribed a Kerryman on the jury to have the jury find him guilty of manslaughter. After being out ten hours, the jury returned a verdict of manslaughter.

'I'll be forever in your debt,' the defendant said to the Kerryman, 'how did you manage it at all?'

'I had a terrible job,' said the Kerryman, 'the other eleven wanted to acquit you.'

☺   ☺   ☺

A Kerryman had a mule whose ears were so long that every time he put him into the stable the mule grazed his ears on the top of the doorway. So the Kerryman decided to knock six inches off the wall over the doorway.

'Why don't you take away the ledge under the door?' asked a friend. 'It would be less dangerous and much less expensive.'

'Look,' said the Kerryman, 'it's the mule's ears that are causing the trouble, not his feet.'

☺   ☺   ☺

Then there was the Kerryman who joined the 75th regiment of the army, to be near his brother who was in the 76th regiment.

☺   ☺   ☺

A Kerryman bought a large engagement ring for his girlfriend.

'Ooh,' she gasped, 'is it a real diamond?'

'If it's not,' said the Kerryman, 'I've just been done out of
€5.'

☺   ☺   ☺

One Kerryman bet another that he couldn't carry him across
Niagara Falls on a tightrope. After a hair-raising trip they
made it to the other side. As one Kerryman handed over the
bet of €1,000 to the other he sighed, 'I was sure I had won
the bet when you wobbled halfway over.'

☺   ☺   ☺

As the *Titanic* was sinking, a Kerryman was swimming madly
round the ship, shouting, 'Where's the dance, where's the
dance?'

'What do you mean "dance"?' asked a drowning passenger.

'I heard an announcement only ten minutes ago,' said the
Kerryman, 'a-band-on-ship, a-band-on-ship.'

☺   ☺   ☺

A Kerryman applied for a job as an RTE newscaster but was
turned down.

'I'll bet I didn't get the job,' he complained, 'just because
I'm a K-K-K-K-Kerryman.'

☺   ☺   ☺

A Kerryman went to the doctor and complained that every
time he drank a cup of tea he got a sharp pain in his eye.

'Have you tried taking the spoon out of the cup?' asked
the doctor.

☺   ☺   ☺

A tailor's iron is called a 'goose'. A Kerry tailor wanted to buy two new irons, so he wrote away to the manufacturers as follows:

'Dear Sir,

Please send me two gooses…'

After reading the letter he decided that this wouldn't do, so he changed it to:

'Dear Sir,

Please send me two geese…'

However, he again felt that there was something wrong and that the manufacturers would be laughing at him. Finally he hit upon the following:

'Dear Sir,

Please send me a goose…

P. S. While you're at it, you may as well send me a second one.'

☺   ☺   ☺

A lady hired a Kerryman to look after her goldfish. One day she asked him if he had changed the water in the goldfish bowl.

'Indeed I haven't,' he replied, 'they didn't drink what I gave them last week.'

☺   ☺   ☺

A Kerryman's brother died, so he decided he would put a death notice in the paper.

'How much does a death notice cost?' he asked the girl at the counter.

'€10 an inch,' she replied.

'I'll never manage to pay,' said the Kerryman, 'my brother was six foot four inches tall.'

☺   ☺   ☺

A fellow played the following trick on a Kerryman.

'Listen,' he said, 'punch me on the hand as hard as you like,' placing his hand up against a brick wall.

The Kerryman swung his fist but at the last moment the fellow pulled away his hand, and the Kerryman's fist went crashing into the brick wall.

After a good laugh, the Kerryman decided to try out the trick on his friend.

'Listen,' he said, 'punch me on the hand as hard as you like.'

He looked around for a wall but he couldn't find one.

'We would really need a brick wall to do this trick properly, but never mind, I'll hold my hand in front of my face.'

☺ ☺ ☺

A Kerryman who fell a hundred feet from a building was asked if the fall had hurt him.

'It wasn't the fall at all,' he replied, 'but the sudden stop.'

'I suppose,' he added after a few minutes' reflection, 'that I was lucky that the ground broke my fall.'

☺ ☺ ☺

A Kerryman was digging a hole in the ground, when a passer-by asked where he was going to put all the clay out of the hole.

'I'll dig another hole,' said the Kerryman.

'But how do you know it will all fit?'

'I'll dig the other hole deeper,' said the Kerryman.

☺ ☺ ☺

A Kerryman nearly became a hero by diving fully clothed into a river to rescue a drowning man. He only made one mistake – he hung the man up to dry on a tree by the river.

A Kerryman's house caught fire, so he rushed to the nearest telephone kiosk and dialled very quickly.

'Hello, is that 999?'

'No, this is 998.'

'Well, would you nip in next door and tell them my house is on fire?'

☺ ☺ ☺

Two Kerrymen were building a house.

'Hey,' said the first Kerryman, 'these nails are defective. The heads are on the wrong end.'

'You fool,' said the second Kerryman, 'those are for the other side of the house.'

☺ ☺ ☺

A Kerryman who went to London had never seen traffic lights before, so he asked a policeman what they were.

'When the lights are red,' said the policeman, 'Englishmen are allowed to proceed, and when they are green Irishmen are allowed to proceed.'

'This is a great country,' said the Kerryman, 'the Orangemen never get a chance.'

☺ ☺ ☺

An American in a pub bet a Kerryman €100 that he couldn't drink ten pints of stout in ten minutes.

'You're on,' said the Kerryman, 'give me a few minutes to prepare myself,' and he vanished out the door. Fifteen minutes later he returned and drank the ten pints of stout in ten minutes.

'I knew I could manage it,' said the Kerryman, 'because I just did it in the pub next door.'

A tourist travelling around Kerry was horrified to see a cart loaded with hay, with two Kerrymen sitting on top, suddenly emerging into the narrow road from a field. He jammed on his brakes, but he couldn't stop in time, so in desperation he drove the car over the roadside hedge and into the field, where it burst into flames.

'Bejabers,' said one Kerryman to the other, 'some of these tourists are terrible drivers. We only just got out of that field in time.'

☺   ☺   ☺

A little Kerry lad asked his mother if he could go outside to watch the eclipse of the sun.

'Yes,' she replied, 'but don't stand too near.'

☺   ☺   ☺

Two Kerrywomen were talking at a bus stop:

'I don't know what to buy my little boy for his birthday,' said the first.

'Why not buy him a book?' asked the second.

'Don't be crazy,' said the first, 'he's got a book already.'

☺   ☺   ☺

A Kerryman, a Corkman and a Clareman were in a queue to buy potatoes outside a grocer's shop.

'Sorry,' said the grocer, 'I'm not serving Corkmen today.' So the Corkman left the queue.

After a while the grocer reappeared and said, 'Sorry, I'm not serving any Claremen today.' So the Clareman departed.

Finally the grocer said, 'Sorry, I have no potatoes at all today.' So the Kerryman said, 'That's just typical, serving the Corkman first.'

A Kerryman was on the boat to Holyhead when there was a shout of 'Man overboard'. The captain shouted 'throw in a buoy', so the Kerryman grabbed a little eight-year-old boy and threw him into the water.

'No, you fool,' said the captain, 'I meant a cork buoy.'

'How the heck was I to know what part of Ireland he was from?' roared the Kerryman.

☺ ☺ ☺

A Kerryman paid €500 to have his car insured against fire.

'For €100 more,' said the agent, 'you can insure it against theft also.'

'That would be a waste of money,' said the Kerryman, 'who would ever steal a burning car?'

☺ ☺ ☺

A fellow was explaining to a Kerryman how nature sometimes compensates for a person's deficiencies.

'For example,' he told him, 'if a man is deaf, he may have keener sight, and if a man is blind, he may have a very keen sense of smell.'

'I think I see what you mean,' said the Kerryman, 'I've often noticed that if a man has one short leg, then the other one is always a little bit longer.'

☺ ☺ ☺

During the Emergency a Kerry regiment was sent to immobilise a railway station. After about five minutes they returned without a single casualty, and carrying a large sack.

'How do you manage to do it so quickly?' asked the commander.

'Easy,' answered the regiment leader. 'We simply stole all the railway tickets.'

A Kerryman visiting the zoo stood in front of the snake-house, putting his tongue out at the snakes.

'What's going on here?' asked a keeper.

'Look,' said the Kerryman, 'they started it.'

☺ ☺ ☺

A Kerryman rushed into an insurance office and said, 'I'd like to buy some house insurance please.'

'Certainly sir,' said the clerk, 'just fill in these forms.'

'I can't wait that long,' said the Kerryman, 'my house is on fire.'

☺ ☺ ☺

A Kerryman arrived up in Dublin and stood looking up at Liberty Hall. A Dubliner arrived on the scene and said, 'Look, you've got to pay me €1 for every storey of Liberty Hall you look up at. How many storeys did you look at?'

'Five,' said the Kerryman, and handed over €5 .

'I certainly fooled him,' said the Kerryman to himself afterwards, 'I really looked at ten storeys.'

☺ ☺ ☺

Having visited all the animals in the zoo, a Kerryman spent half an hour looking for the Exit, but finally decided that it must have escaped.

☺ ☺ ☺

Two Kerrymen lost on a dark night came upon a milestone.

'We must have wandered into a graveyard,' said the first.

'Some fellow called "Miles from Dublin" is buried in this grave,' said the second.

'You're right,' said the first, 'look at the age he was – 175.'

Kerry sergeant to his regiment during a battle: 'Keep firing, men, and don't let the enemy know that we are out of ammunition.'

☺ ☺ ☺

A Kerryman went into a shop and asked for four dozen mothballs.

'But,' said the shop assistant, 'you bought four dozen mothballs only yesterday.'

'That's right,' said the Kerryman, 'but those damn moths are very hard to hit.'

☺ ☺ ☺

A Kerryman went to London and found himself in the Underground late one night. Seeing a notice 'Dogs must be carried on the escalator', he moaned to himself, 'Where am I going to find a dog at this hour of the night?'

☺ ☺ ☺

A Kerryman was suffering from pains in his knees, so he visited the doctor.

'You're suffering from a disease that we medical experts call "kneeitis",' said the doctor. 'Take it easy for a month or so and above all don't climb any stairs. That puts a terrible strain on the knees.'

A month later the Kerryman returned and after a brief examination was found to have recovered completely.

'Can I climb the stairs now, doctor?'

'Certainly,' replied the doctor.

'Thank Heavens,' said the Kerryman. 'I was getting a bit browned off climbing up the drainpipe every time I wanted to go to the toilet.'

A Kerryman who kept all his money in a mattress was asked why he didn't keep it in the bank, in view of all the interest he would receive.

'I've thought of that too,' said the Kerryman, 'I put a little away every week for the interest as well.'

☺   ☺   ☺

A fellow hired a Kerryman to milk his cows. One morning he found him forcing a cow to drink its own milk from a bucket.

'What the hell are you doing?' he shouted.

'I thought it looked a bit thin,' said the Kerryman, 'so I'm running it through again.'

☺   ☺   ☺

A Kerryman once went to England looking for a job with Weetabix the builder.

☺   ☺   ☺

Two Kerrymen were visiting the cinema for the first time. When they arrived the film had already started, so it was quite dark. As they walked down the aisle they were followed by the usherette with a torch.

'Watch out,' said one Kerryman to the other, 'here comes a bicycle.'

☺   ☺   ☺

Two Kerrymen went on a holiday to France and stayed at a country farmhouse. They were disgusted to find that everybody in France, even the kids, spoke French. One morning they were awoken by a cock crowing.

'Do you know,' said one Kerryman to the other, 'that's the first word of English we've heard spoken since we arrived.'

A Kerryman got a job commanding a fire brigade. One night the brigade was called to a small fire. The Kerryman shouted out, 'Hold it a minute and let it burn up a bit so we can see what we're doing.'

☺ ☺ ☺

Two Kerrymen were watching a John Wayne film on television. In one scene John Wayne was riding madly towards a cliff.

'I bet you €10 that he falls over the cliff,' said one Kerryman to the other.

'Done,' said the second.

John Wayne rode straight over the cliff.

As the second Kerryman handed over his €10, the first said 'I feel a bit guilty about this. I've seen the film before.'
'So have I,' said the second Kerryman, 'but I didn't think he'd be fool enough to make the same mistake twice.'

☺ ☺ ☺

A Kerryman was sick and tired of people heartily slapping him on the back when they met him, so he devised a plan. He put half a dozen sticks of dynamite under his jacket and said, 'There! The next fellow who slaps me on the back will have his stupid arm blown off.'

☺ ☺ ☺

A Kerryman got a job as an electrician and his first assignment was to mend a broken doorbell for an old lady.

After an hour, he returned to his employer and reported, 'The old lady wasn't in. I rang the bell three or four times, but there was no reply.'

☺ ☺ ☺

Two Kerrymen were passing by a nudist colony, so they decided to peep in over the wall and see what was going on inside. So one Kerryman stood on the other's shoulders.

'Are there men and women there?' asked the lower Kerryman.

'I can't tell,' said the upper Kerryman, 'they've no clothes on.'

☺   ☺   ☺

A Kerryman boasted that he had an axe that had lasted over a hundred years. It had been fitted with only five new heads and eight new handles.

☺   ☺   ☺

A world famous symphony orchestra once arrived in a small Kerry village, to give a concert. At the interval, the conductor complained that the acoustics in the little hall were terrible. 'I know,' said the owner of the hall, 'I've tried everything, I've even put down traps, but I can't shift them'.

☺   ☺   ☺

'Which side of the river has the most traffic?' asked a Kerry councillor.

'The north side,' answered his clerk.

'Good,' said the councillor, 'that's the side we'll build the bridge on.'

☺   ☺   ☺

A railway passenger asked a Kerryman what time the next train for Dublin was leaving at.

'The next train for Dublin,' said the Kerryman, 'has just left.'

Announcement in a Kerry army camp: The parade will take place on Sunday afternoon. If the afternoon is wet the parade will take place on Sunday morning.

☺   ☺   ☺

What constitutes a seven course meal for a Kerryman?
    A six-pack and a boiled potato.

☺   ☺   ☺

A Kerryman complained that his wife spent very little time at home.
    'For every once she comes in,' he continued, 'she goes out ten times.'

☺   ☺   ☺

Kerryman viewing a broken window: 'It's worse than I thought. It's broken on both sides.'

☺   ☺   ☺

On seeing a flat tyre on his car, a Kerryman consoled himself by saying that at least it was only flat at the bottom.

☺   ☺   ☺

Two Kerrymen were out fishing. 'This is a marvellous spot for fishing,' said the first, 'how will we find it again?'
    'Don't worry,' said the second, 'I've put a mark on the side of the boat'.
    'You fool,' said the first, 'we might not get this boat the next time.'

☺   ☺   ☺

Have you heard about the Kerryman who pulled a fast one on the Post Office?

He bought 10,000 50c stamps before the postal charges went up.

☺ ☺ ☺

Two Kerryman attended a performance by the world's leading blind pianist.

'It wouldn't matter to him if he wasn't blind,' remarked one Kerryman afterwards.

'How do you make that out?' asked the other Kerryman.

'Well, I kept a close eye on him all evening and he never looks at the piano anyway.'

☺ ☺ ☺

A Kerryman was working on the railroad, when suddenly a train came speeding down the track. The Kerryman took off down the track but was knocked down and badly injured. When he regained consciousness in hospital, the doctor asked him why he had not run up the embankment.

'Don't be a fool,' said the Kerryman, 'if I couldn't out-run it on the flat, what chance had I running uphill?'

☺ ☺ ☺

Two Kerrymen were travelling by train. All of a sudden an express train passed going the other way.

'By jove,' said one Kerryman to the other, 'that was a close shave.'

☺ ☺ ☺

What do you find off the coast of Kerry?

Underwater lighthouses for the submarines.

Kerry workman to his workmate: 'Don't come down that ladder, Mick, I've just taken it away.'

☺ ☺ ☺

A Kerryman went to a psychiatrist to get some help for his wife.

'She's got a morbid fear of having her clothes stolen, doc,' he told the psychiatrist. 'Only two days ago I went home early and found that she had hired a fellow to stay in the wardrobe and guard them.'

☺ ☺ ☺

A Cork girl wanted to marry a Kerryman, but her parents refused to give their consent. The lovers decided to commit suicide by jumping off the Cliffs of Moher. Only the girl hit the water, however. The Kerryman got lost on the way down.

☺ ☺ ☺

A Kerryman was being treated for years by the doctor for lumbago. Just as the treatment had taken effect, the Kerryman died of a rare tropical disease – frostbite.

'At least,' the doctor consoled his widow,' you have the consolation of knowing he died cured.'

☺ ☺ ☺

Have you heard about the Kerryman who went into a posh restaurant?

He ordered an expensive four-course meal, paid for it, and then sneaked out without eating it.

☺ ☺ ☺

There were ninety-eight Kerrymen jammed into a bus, so the conductor called out 'There's no need for all this crush, there's another bus behind'. So the ninety-eight Kerrymen got out of the first bus and jammed into the bus behind.

☺   ☺   ☺

A tourist travelling in Kerry ordered coffee without cream in a cafe.

'We haven't a drop of cream in the house, sir,' said the waitress, 'would it do if I served you coffee without milk?'

☺   ☺   ☺

A Kerryman was selling his cow at the market.

'She'll give milk year after year without having a calf,' he told a prospective buyer, 'because she came of a cow that never had a calf.'

☺   ☺   ☺

A Kerryman bought a watch at a sale but returned a few days later and complained that the watch lost fifteen minutes in each hour.

'Of course it does,' said the jeweller, 'my sign says, "All watches 25% off".'

☺   ☺   ☺

Two Kerrymen each had a horse, but they couldn't tell them apart. So the first cut the tail off his horse, and all went well for a while. But then the second Kerryman's horse lost its tail in an accident, so they were back where they started. Finally, they consulted a wise man in the village where they lived and he said: 'Can't you two fools see that the black horse is three inches taller than the white horse?'

A Kerryman arrived up at work over four hours late.

'What excuse do you have this time?' asked the boss.

'The trouble with me,' said the Kerryman, 'is that I sleep very slowly.'

☺ ☺ ☺

It is not widely known that God at first intended to have His son born in Kerry. There was only one snag – He couldn't find three wise men.

☺ ☺ ☺

A doctor told a Kerryman to give his wife as much sleeping powder as would cover a 10 cent piece. When the doctor called a week later to see his patient the Kerryman said: 'She's been sleeping for over six days!'

'Did you give her the sleeping powder exactly as I prescribed?' asked the doctor.

'Not exactly,' said the Kerryman, 'I didn't have a 10 cent piece so I used five two cent pieces instead.'

☺ ☺ ☺

A Kerryman was giving a lecture on archaeology. 'Look at some of the cities of antiquity,' he exclaimed, 'some of them have perished so utterly that it is doubtful whether they ever existed.'

☺ ☺ ☺

Two Kerrymen had been lying in wait for over three hours in order to ambush their sworn enemy. Finally one Kerryman turned to the other and said, 'He's late. I hope to God nothing has happened to the poor fellow.'

A Kerryman was reporting to the guards that his wife had gone swimming over a month previously, and hadn't returned. He was now worried that she had drowned.

'Did she have any distinguishing features?' asked the sergeant.

'She spoke with a pronounced stutter,' said the Kerryman.

☺   ☺   ☺

A rocket on its way to the moon contained a Kerryman and a monkey, each having his instructions in a sealed envelope. When the monkey opened his envelope he read: 1. Check oxygen levels in lunar module. 2. Prepare retrorockets for minor course adjustments. 3. Examine all technical apparatus and efficiency levels. When the Kerryman opened his envelope his instructions read: Feed the monkey.

☺   ☺   ☺

A Corkman and a Kerryman were boasting about the advanced technology that had been used by their respective ancestors.

'During a recent excavation of an ancient Cork castle,' said the Corkman, 'miles of cable were discovered, proving that Corkmen were using the telegraph hundreds of years ago.'

'That's nothing,' said the Kerryman, 'underneath an ancient Kerry castle they found no cable at all, proving that Kerrymen were communicating with each other by radio, when Corkmen were still using the telegraph.'

☺   ☺   ☺

Two Kerrymen were in a space rocket. The first left the rocket on a space walk, and when he returned he knocked on the capsule door.

'Who's there?' asked the second Kerryman.

Two Kerrymen went to Dublin for the weekend, and in a high-spirited moment took a double-decker bus for a joy ride. They crashed into a low bridge and made smithereens of the bus. When they appeared in court, the judge asked them why they had not stolen a single-decker bus, in view of all the low bridges they would meet.

'It's my friend here,' said one Kerryman, pointing to the other, 'he likes to go upstairs for a smoke.'

☺   ☺   ☺

One Kerryman met another carrying a bag on his back.

'What's in the bag?' asked the first Kerryman.

'I won't tell you,' said the second.

'Go on, do.'

'All right then, it's ducks.'

'If I guess how many ducks you have in the bag, will you give me one of them?'

'Look,' said the second Kerryman, 'if you guess the correct number, I'll give you both of them.'

'Five,' said the first Kerryman.

'How did you guess?' said the second Kerryman.

☺   ☺   ☺

A Kerryman went to Dublin to earn his living as a con man. He didn't fare too well, however. The first fellow to whom he tried to sell O'Connell Bridge turned out to be the owner and the Kerryman had to give him €50 to stop him reporting the incident to the guards.

☺   ☺   ☺

A Kerryman told a friend that he hadn't a living relative in the world except a cousin who died four years ago in America.

A Kerryman on a building site was working at a furious rate, carrying a huge load of bricks up a ladder every thirty seconds.

'Why are you working so hard?' asked his mate.

'I've got them all fooled,' grinned the Kerryman, 'I'm carrying the same load of bricks up all the time.'

☺   ☺   ☺

A Kerryman was boasting about his brother's exploits in the army.

'He was the finest soldier of the day,' he claimed. 'Although he had only one arm, he used to rush into battle without a single weapon. His favourite method of disposing of the enemy was by banging their heads together.'

'How could he bang their heads together if he had only one arm?' asked a listener.

'In the heat of the battle,' replied the Kerryman, 'my brother forgot all about that.'

☺   ☺   ☺

A Kerry town had just provided a beautiful ornamental lake for its town park. One councillor proposed that they buy a gondola and place it on the lake.

'I've a better idea,' said a second councillor, 'why not buy two gondolas, a male and a female, and let nature take its course?'

☺   ☺   ☺

First Kerryman: 'How much did the garage charge for towing your car home from Dublin?'
Second Kerryman: '€500.'
First Kerryman: 'That was a bit steep wasn't it?'
Second Kerryman: 'I made them earn every penny of it. I kept the hand-brake on all the way.'

A lady hired three Kerrymen to move her furniture. When she saw two of them struggling to carry a wardrobe upstairs, she asked where the third was.

'Oh he's in the wardrobe stopping the wire coat-hangers from rattling.'

☺   ☺   ☺

Two Kerrymen bought new Volkswagens and went for a drive. The first Kerryman's Volkswagen broke down so the second stopped to investigate.

'I've looked under the bonnet,' said the first Kerryman, 'and there seems to be no engine.'

'Don't worry,' said the second Kerryman, 'I've got a spare in my boot.'

☺   ☺   ☺

The captain of a ship told the mate, a Kerryman of course, to proceed to room 36 and arrange to have the occupant, who had died during the night, buried at sea.

An hour later the mate reported, 'I proceeded to room 26 and had the occupant buried at sea, as requested sir.'

'My God,' said the captain, 'I said room 36. Who was the occupant of room 26?'

'A Corkman, sir.'

'Was he dead?'

'Well, he said he wasn't. But you know these Corkmen – they're all terrible liars.'

☺   ☺   ☺

On the first night of their honeymoon, a Kerryman confessed to his bride that he had a major deficiency – he was 100% colour-blind.

She replied, 'You sho am dat honey, you sho am dat.'

A Kerryman joined the New York police force and was given a patrol car to drive. The climax of his career came when he gave chase to the most wanted gang of criminals in the city, in his patrol car. Unfortunately, he noticed from his mile-ometer that the 20,000 miles were up, so he had to pull into the garage for an oil change.

A Kerryman complained to his landlady that his blanket was still too short, despite the fact that he had cut several strips off the top and sewn them onto the bottom.

A Kerryman got a job as a lumberjack, but try as he might, he couldn't meet his quota of fifty trees a day. By chance he saw an ad in a shop window for chain saws 'guaranteed to fell 60 trees a day'. So he bought one, but the best he could manage was 40 trees a day.

So he took it back to the shop and complained that there must be something wrong with it.

'Let me look at it,' said the man in the shop. So he took the chain saw and switched it on.

'What's that noise?' said the Kerryman.

A Kerryman working on a building site woke up one morning three hours late for work. In his haste, he unwittingly put his trousers on back to front. Later that day he fell fifty feet from the scaffolding and lay on the ground. As the ambulance arrived the foreman asked him if he was badly injured.

'I don't rightly know,' said the Kerryman, eyeing his trousers for the first time, 'but I've certainly given myself one hell of a twist.'

This fellow was given an €18 note so he tried to change it in several banks but was quickly thrown out. Finally he tried a bank owned by a Kerryman.

'Certainly I'll change it,' said the Kerryman. 'How would you like it, two nines or three sixes?'

☺   ☺   ☺

Two Kerrymen were having a nap on a building site.

'These pipes make terribly hard pillows,' said one.

'Why don't you do as I've done?' said the second, 'I've stuffed mine with straw.'

☺   ☺   ☺

A Kerryman on his first aeroplane flight was offered some chewing gum by the stewardess.

'What's that for?' he asked.

'It's to protect your ears during take-off,' she replied.

Some time later she asked him how he was feeling.

'What's that?' he said.

'How are you feeling now?' she shouted.

'I'm sorry,' s aid the Kerryman, 'I can't hear a word you're saying with all this chewing gum in my ears.'

☺   ☺   ☺

A Kerryman wrote the following letter to the editor of a newspaper:

'Dear Sir,

Last week I lost my gold pocket watch, so yesterday I put an ad in your "Lost and Found" columns. Last night I found the watch in the trousers of my other suit. God Bless your newspaper.'

☺   ☺   ☺

'I'm glad I don't like cabbage,' said a Kerryman, ' because if I liked it I'd eat lots of it, and I can't stand the sight of the stuff.'

☺   ☺   ☺

One Kerryman met another at the races.

'I've just pulled a fast one on the bookies,' grinned the first Kerryman, 'I'm bound to have the winner in the next race.'

'How can you be certain?' asked the second Kerryman.

'I've put €10 on every one of the horses in the race.'

☺   ☺   ☺

Two Kerrymen were flying home from London in a four engine jet. Suddenly the following announcement came over the intercom: 'Ladies and Gentlemen; one of the engines has failed and we will be an hour late in arriving.'

A few minutes later it was announced that another engine had failed and that there would be a delay of three hours. Finally it was announced that a third engine had failed and that there would be a delay of six hours in arriving.

One Kerryman turned to the other and said, 'If that fourth engine goes, we will be up here all night.'

☺   ☺   ☺

A Kerryman got a job as an assistant gardener at a big country house. One day he saw a bird bath for the first time.

'What's that for?' he asked the head gardener.

'That's a bird bath,' he replied

'I don't believe you,' said the Kerryman, 'there isn't a bird in creation who can tell the difference between Saturday night and any other night of the week.'

☺   ☺   ☺

A Kerryman on a trip to London picked up two books called *How to Hug* and *From Sex to Sin*. He smuggled them in past the customs but, when he arrived home, he found that he had bought two odd volumes of an old encyclopaedia.

☺ ☺ ☺

During the war a Kerryman joined the air force and was detailed to disperse 100,000 propaganda leaflets all over Germany. He returned to base over six months later, in an exhausted condition.

'Where on earth have you been?' asked his commander, 'surely it doesn't take six months to drop a few leaflets.'

'Drop them?' said the Kerryman, 'I thought you wanted me to put them under all the doors.'

☺ ☺ ☺

'You have been found not guilty of robbery,' said the judge to the Kerryman.

'Does that mean I can keep the money?'

☺ ☺ ☺

One Kerryman was telling another of his plans to make a lot of money.

'I intend to buy a dozen swarms of bees and every morning at dawn I'm going to let them into the park opposite where I live to spend all day making honey, while I relax.'

'But the park doesn't open until nine o'clock,' protested the second Kerryman.

'I realise that,' said the first Kerryman, 'but I know where there is a hole in the fence.'

☺ ☺ ☺

A Kerryman was sentenced to be shot by a firing squad, so he was asked if he wanted to make a last request.

'No,' he replied, 'There's nothing I want.'

'How about a cigarette?'

'No,' said the Kerryman, 'I'm trying to give them up.'

☺   ☺   ☺

A Kerryman visited his psychiatrist and said, 'Look doc, I've got two questions to ask you.'

'Right,' said the psychiatrist, 'ask me the first question'.

'Doc,' said the Kerryman, 'could I possibly be in love with an elephant?'

'Of course not,' said the psychiatrist, 'what's your other question?'

'Do you know of anybody who wants to buy a very large engagement ring?'

☺   ☺   ☺

A Kerryman on his way home on a dark night fell into a drain by the roadside. He waved his fist up at the sky and shouted in disgust, 'Blast you for a moon, you'd be out on a bright night.'

☺   ☺   ☺

'Did you get as much as you expected for your cow?' a neighbour asked a Kerryman on his way home from the market.

'I didn't get as much as I expected,' said the Kerryman, 'but then I didn't expect I would.'

☺   ☺   ☺

Did you hear about the Kerryman who took his car for a service?

He couldn't get it in the church door.

A Kerryman on a visit to Dublin, asked a guard what time it was.

'A quarter past three,' answered the guard.

'This is a crazy city,' said the Kerryman, 'I've been asking people all day and I've got a different answer every time.'

☺   ☺   ☺

A fellow wanted to have his house renovated, but thought that all the estimates he received were too high. Finally he consulted a Kerry contractor who came to view his house.

'I'll completely redecorate your bedroom for €150,' said the Kerryman.

'Great', said the fellow, 'all the others wanted at least €1,000.'

At this the Kerryman rushed over to the window and shouted out 'Green side up, green side up.'

'How about the bathroom?' asked the fellow, 'the others wanted at least €2,500.'

'My men and I will do it for €50.17,' said the Kerryman, whereupon he rushed to the window and shouted 'Green side up, green side up.'

'Well you seem to be the man I've been looking for,' said the fellow, 'just tell me one thing, why do you go to the window and shout, "Green side up, green side up?"'

'That's just technical information to my workmen,' said the Kerrymen, 'they're laying a lawn next door.'

☺   ☺   ☺

A Kerryman was lost in a big city, so he asked a passer-by where the other side of the street was.

'Why it's over there,' said the passer-by, pointing to the other side of the street.

'That's funny,' said the Kerryman, 'I was over there a few minutes ago and they told me it was over here'.

A Kerryman's house went on fire, so he phoned the fire brigade and told them to come at once.

'Have you been doing anything to quench the blaze?' asked the fire chief.

'Yes,' said the Kerryman, 'I've been pouring water on it.'

'Well there's no point in us coming over,' said the fire chief, 'that's all we can do.'

☺   ☺   ☺

A tourist staying at a Kerry hotel was awakened at 6.30 a.m. by a porter who sang out: 'A parcel for you sir, just arrived in the post.'

'Let it wait until after breakfast,' shouted the angry guest.

At about 7.15 the same guest was disturbed by the same porter who shouted out: 'That parcel sir. It wasn't for you after all.'

☺   ☺   ☺

Two Kerrymen were out duck shooting. The first Kerryman took aim, fired, and shot down a duck which landed at his feet.

'You could have saved the shot,' said the second Kerryman, 'the fall would have killed it anyway.'

☺   ☺   ☺

Two Kerrymen were walking along a railway line at night.

'This is a heck of a long flight of stairs,' said the first.

'It's not the number of steps that worries me,' said the second, 'it's the low railings.'

☺   ☺   ☺

A Kerrywoman heard her young son using a number of words and phrases that she considered objectionable.

'Who did you get those words from?' she asked him.

'I got them from Shakespeare, mother,' he replied.

'Well don't ever play with him again.'

☺   ☺   ☺

A Kerryman who became a barrister once stated in court: 'Your honour, the offence was committed at a quarter past twelve at night on the morning of the next day.'

☺   ☺   ☺

A dangerous criminal had escaped, so the police issued the usual photographs: left profile, front view and right profile. A few days later they received the following telegram from a Kerry detective: 'Have captured the fellow on the left, and the fellow in the middle, and at the rate I'm going it won't be long before I get the fellow on the right as well.'

☺   ☺   ☺

A Kerryman went to the doctor and complained of a severe pain in his stomach.

'Have you eaten anything unusual recently?' asked the doctor.

'I had oysters for dinner yesterday,' said the Kerryman.

'Were they fresh?'

'I don't know.'

'What do you mean you don't know?' asked the doctor, 'surely you examined them before you removed the shells?'

'Nobody told me that you had to remove the shells,' said the Kerryman.

☺   ☺   ☺

A Kerryman got a job as an electrician's assistant. 'Here,' said the electrician one day, 'grab one of these two wires. Do you feel anything?'

'No,' said the Kerryman.

'Well don't touch the other wire. It's got 10,000 volts in it.'

☺ ☺ ☺

What do you call a Kerryman with one ear?
Half blind.
What do you call a Kerryman with no ears?
Totally blind.
(This joke is for honours students – if you want a clue, think of what happens to the Kerryman's cap).

☺ ☺ ☺

A Kerryman was asked how he was getting on with a pair of rubber gloves that he had purchased.

'They are terrific,' he replied, 'if you put them on, you can wash your hands without them getting wet'.

☺ ☺ ☺

Have you heard about the two Kerrymen who were caught stealing a calendar?

They each got six months.

☺ ☺ ☺

A Kerryman was challenged to fight a duel, so he accepted under certain conditions.

'What are the conditions?' asked his opponent.

'Well,' said the Kerryman, 'can I stand nearer to you, than you are to me, since I've lost the sight of one eye entirely?'

A Kerry sergeant was teaching two young recruits to march, with very little success. Finally in despair he shouted at them: 'If I knew which one of you fools was out of step, I'd put him in the guard-house.'

☺ ☺ ☺

A businessman hired a Kerry girl as his private secretary. One day he asked her to find the telephone number of Mr Zimmerman. About an hour later he asked her if she had found it yet.

'I'm bound to find it soon,' she told him, 'I've worked my way right through the telephone directory as far as the letter T.'

☺ ☺ ☺

A doctor, having prescribed an emetic for a Kerryman, received the following letter from him:

'My dear doctor,

That emetic you gave me was worse than useless. I tried it twice but I couldn't keep it in my stomach either time.'

☺ ☺ ☺

A Kerryman and an American were sitting in the bar at Shannon airport.

'I've come to meet my brother,' said the Kerryman, 'he's due to fly in from America in an hour's time. It's his first trip home in forty years.'

'Will you be able to recognise him?' asked the American.

'I'm sure I won't,' said the Kerryman, 'after all that time.'

'I wonder if he will recognise you?' said the American.

'Of course he will,' said the Kerryman, 'sure I haven't been away at all.'

An American tourist travelling in Kerry came across a little antique shop in which he was lucky enough to pick up, for a mere €150, the skull of Brian Boru. Included in the price was a certificate of the skull's authenticity, signed by Brian Boru himself.

Ten years later the tourist returned to Ireland and asked the little Kerryman who owned the antique shop if he had any more bargains.

'I've got the very thing for you' said the Kerryman, 'it's the genuine skull of Brian Boru.'

'You swindler,' said the American, 'you sold me that ten years ago,' and producing the skull added, 'look, they're not even the same size'.

'You have it all wrong,' said the Kerryman, 'this is the skull of Brian Boru when he was a lad.'

☺   ☺   ☺

Here is a sad little story about a Kerrywoman who tried to wash the floor.

She broke her washing machine.

☺   ☺   ☺

A Kerryman who became a literary critic once claimed that Shakespeare's plays were not written by Shakespeare, but by another gentleman of the same name.

☺   ☺   ☺

A homesick Kerryman in a Birmingham dole queue, asked the man next to him if he was from Kerry.

'Look,' said the fellow, 'it's bad enough being black.'

☺   ☺   ☺

A school inspector travelling in Kerry, asked a young boy in class: 'Who knocked down the walls of Jericho?'

'It wasn't me, sir,' said the boy nervously.

Furious with the low standard in the class, the inspector reported the incident to the headmaster of the school.

'I asked a young lad, who knocked down the walls of Jericho, and he told me that it wasn't him.'

'The little rascal,' said the headmaster, 'I bet it was him all the time.'

Even more furious, the inspector went to the school manager and repeated the story.

'Well,' said the school manager, 'the boy comes from an honest family, and you can take it from me, that if he says he didn't knock down the walls of Jericho, then he is telling the truth.'

Finally, in despair, the inspector reported the whole affair to the Department of Education. He received the following communication:

'Dear Sir,

With regard to your recent letter concerning the Walls of Jericho we beg to inform you that this matter does not fall within the jurisdiction of this department. We therefore suggest that you refer the problem to the Board of Works.'

☺   ☺   ☺

Oil has just been discovered off the coast of Kerry. There's only one snag – it's too thick to pump ashore.

☺   ☺   ☺

There was this Kerryman who was very self-centred and always wanted to be the focus of attention. If he went to a funeral he would want to be the corpse!

A man with an alligator on a lead walked into a bar.

'Do you serve Sligomen in here?' he roared.

'Yes, of course we do,' said the terrified barman.

'Good, I'll have two for the alligator.'

A member of the Offaly football team arrived home after a match with a leg that was black, blue and bruised.

'Aren't you worried?' asked his wife.

'Yes, I don't even know whose leg it is'.

A Wicklowman applied to have his name included in 'Who's Who'.

He was turned down, but they offered instead to put his picture in 'What's This?'

Two Corkmen, one very thin and the other very fat, fell from the top of a high building. Which one hit the ground first?

Who cares, so long as they are both Corkmen.

☺   ☺   ☺

A Kerryman was boasting about his son, 'He's one of the cleverest lads in the country,' he told a friend, 'he's always helping the police with their enquiries.'

☺   ☺   ☺

Two Kerrymen were talking part in a hairy bacon eating contest in West Cork. The local champion was expected to sweep the boards but he was stopped in his tracks when the first Kerryman said to the other, 'Will we cook it or what?'

☺   ☺   ☺

A Kerryman went to his doctor and asked him to give him something for the wind.

The doctor gave him a kite.

☺ ☺ ☺

This Kerryman went into a post restaurant with his wife and ordered an expensive bottle of wine.

'Certainly, sir,' said the waiter, 'which year?'

'I'll have it right away,' said the Kerryman, 'if you don't mind!'

☺ ☺ ☺

A Kerryman went into hospital for an operation and woke up shouting, 'Doctor, doctor, I can't feel my legs!'

'I know,' said the doctor, 'I've just cut your arms off.'

☺ ☺ ☺

A Kerryman broke into the gambling casino at Las Vegas. When the police caught him he was $3,000 down.

☺ ☺ ☺

A newspaper once published the following retraction of a Kerry news item:

'Instead of being jailed for murdering his wife by pushing her downstairs and throwing a lighting oil lamp after her as we reported last week, we believe that the Reverend Roger MacIntosh in fact died unmarried four years ago.'

☺ ☺ ☺

Have you heard about the Kerry nightclub that employed a chucker-in?

Two Kerrymen were waiting as a bus came along.

'Is this a one-man bus?' the first Kerryman asked the driver.

'It is,' replied the driver.

'We'll wait for the next one,' said the second Kerryman, 'because we both want to get on.'

☺ ☺ ☺

A Kerryman was the oldest man in Ireland and had reached the remarkable age of a hundred and twenty years. A national newspaper sent their top reporter to interview him on the occasion of his birthday.

'To what do you attribute your great age?' the reporter asked him.

'To the fact that it is so long since I was born,' said the Kerryman with a twinkle in his eye.

'Let us be serious,' said the reporter, 'why have you lived to a hundred and twenty?'

'Vitamin pills,' said the Kerryman, 'I've been taking a vitamin pill every day since I was a hundred and ten.'

☺ ☺ ☺

Have you heard about the Kerryman who was a trade union dentist?

His motto was 'one out–all out'.

☺ ☺ ☺

First Kerryman: 'The clock goes back this week.'
Second Kerryman: 'You should have kept up with the repayments.'

☺ ☺ ☺

This Kerryman went to the doctor and told him that he needed some medical attention.

'What seems to be the problem?' asked the doctor.

'Well, doc,' said the Kerryman, 'it's just that I go to the toilet regularly at seven o'clock every morning.'

'That's splendid,' said the doctor, 'why should you be worried about that?'

'I don't get up until eight o'clock,' said the Kerryman.

☺   ☺   ☺

A Kerryman went to the dentist and asked him to take all his teeth out.

'All of them?' said the dentist.

'Yes,' said the Kerryman, 'all of them.'

So the dentist took out all the Kerryman's teeth.

'April fool,' said the Kerryman, 'all I have is a sore finger.'

Afterwards a friend asked him what it was like having all his teeth out.

'Never again,' said the Kerryman, 'never again.'

☺   ☺   ☺

A Kerryman applied for a job as head book-keeper with a big firm and was being interviewed by the top directors of the company.

'So you would like to become our head book-keeper, would you?' asked one director.

'That's right,' said the Kerryman, 'I would indeed.'

'And tell me,' said the director, 'what experience have you?'

'A lot of experience,' said the Kerryman, 'I have two library books that are overdue for over six months.'

☺   ☺   ☺

Have you heard about the Kerryman who has six O levels? He had O in mathematics, O in science, O in geography, O in history, O in Latin and O in French.

☺ ☺ ☺

This fellow went into a garage owned by a Kerryman and asked him to check the tyres. The Kerryman walked around the car, kicked each of the tyres in turn and said to him: 'You're fine, you have four of them.'

☺ ☺ ☺

A Kerryman went to a psychiatrist and told him he was having some problems.

'Describe your symptoms to me,' said the psychiatrist.

'Sometimes I feel I am a wigwam,' said the Kerryman, 'and sometimes I feel I'm a tepee.'

'You're too tense,' said the psychiatrist.

☺ ☺ ☺

News item: Late last night a Kerryman fell into an upholstery machine. Latest reports say he is now fully recovered.

☺ ☺ ☺

A Kerryman was being interviewed for the post of chief accountant and financial officer for a big company and he made a big impression on the board of directors.

'Well,' said the chairman of the board, 'we have decided to appoint you to the position at an annual salary of €100,000.'

'That's great,' said the Kerryman, 'how much a week does that work out at?'

☺ ☺ ☺

A Kerryman was before the court charged with driving his car at over a hundred miles an hour.

'What is your excuse?' asked the judge.

'Look, your worship,' said the Kerryman, 'I do everything very quickly.'

'Let's see how quickly you can do fourteen days,' said the judge.

☺   ☺   ☺

Two Kerrymen were drinking late one night and found themselves stranded in town at midnight without even a taxi fare.

'I'll tell you what,' said the first, 'let's break into the bus garage and steal a number 10.'

'Right,' said the second, so after about half an hour of the most ferocious banging and crashing he emerged with a number 8 explaining that all the number 10s were all at the back.

'Couldn't you have taken a number 14 and we could have got off at the supermarket,' hissed the first Kerryman, 'now I'll go down to the bus stop and you pick me up there.'

But the second Kerryman whizzed past the bus stop and when his friend arrived home an hour later wet and exhausted he explained, 'it was a request stop and you didn't put your hand out.'

☺   ☺   ☺

A Kerryman went into a hardware shop and asked the assistant if he had long nails (no, not the old 'scratch my back' joke).

'Certainly, sir,' said the assistant, 'how long do you want them?'

'I want to keep them,' said the Kerryman.

☺   ☺   ☺

A Kerryman went to the doctor and told him he was having some digestive trouble.

'What have you been eating?' asked the doctor.

'Snooker balls,' said the Kerryman.

'How many do you eat every day?'

'About a dozen,' said the Kerryman. 'I have three reds for breakfast, a blue and a black for lunch, followed by a brown and a blue, three reds for dinner, and a yellow and a pink for tea.'

'That's your trouble,' said the doctor, 'you're not eating any greens.'

☺   ☺   ☺

This fellow went into a pub and seated at the bar was a Kerryman with the biggest dog he had ever seen.

'Does your dog bite, sir?' he asked the Kerryman.

'No,' said the Kerryman, 'my dog is as gentle as a lamb.'

So the fellow went over and patted the dog and the dog nearly bit his arm off.

'I thought you told me your dog didn't bite,' he screamed at the Kerryman.

'That's right,' said the Kerryman, 'but that's not my dog.'

☺   ☺   ☺

A Kerryman rang the police and asked if they could come and help him.

'What's the trouble, sir?' asked the policeman.

'I've locked my keys in the car,' said the Kerryman.

'We'll be round right away, sir,' said the policeman.

'Please hurry,' said the Kerryman, 'it's pouring rain and I've left the sun-roof open.'

☺   ☺   ☺

A Kerry plumber was on a world tour and on the second week of the tour he was being shown around North America. The highlight of the visit was a trip to Niagara Falls.

'What do you think of that?' asked the guide, waiting for the amazed reaction.

'If I hadn't left my bag of tools at home,' said the Kerryman, 'I could fix the leak that's causing that.'

A bit taken aback, the guide continued, 'I'll have you know that a billion gallons of water fall over the edge every day.'

'Sure why wouldn't it?' said the Kerryman, 'what's to hinder it?'

☺   ☺   ☺

What do you give an eighty-year-old Kerryman who marries an eighteen-year-old girl?

Jump leads.

☺   ☺   ☺

A Kerryman walked into a clothing store and asked to see the cheapest suit in the shop.

'You're wearing it, sir,' said the assistant.

☺   ☺   ☺

A Kerryman received an emergency phone call at work that his house had been blown away in a hurricane.

'It couldn't have,' said the Kerryman, 'I have the key right here in my pocket.'

☺   ☺   ☺

A Kerryman was having problems with his weight so his doctor advised him to do some jogging.

'How much should I jog?' the Kerryman asked.

'About ten miles a day,' said the doctor, 'and ring me in a week.' After a week the Kerryman rang to say he was getting on fine with his jogging but that he was seventy miles from home.

☺   ☺   ☺

A Kerryman joined the army and was being interviewed by an officer to see what regiment he was suitable for.

'Can you fire a gun?' asked the officer.

'No,' said the Kerryman.

'What can you do?' asked the officer.

'I can take messages, sir,' said the Kerryman.

'Good,' said the officer. 'I think we will assign you to the pigeon corps in charge of vital messages being carried to the front by pigeons.'

The Kerryman underwent a week's intensive training in the pigeon corps and on his first morning on the job a pigeon arrived from the front bearing a message.

'Quick,' said the officer, 'go and see what the message is.'

About an hour later the Kerryman returned, bleeding and torn and covered in feathers and pigeon droppings.

'Well,' said the officer, 'what was the message?'

'Coo, coo,' said the Kerryman.

☺   ☺   ☺

The general manager of a large banking group was travelling around the country incognito checking up on the efficiency of his branches. He came to a little branch in Kerry where the bank was closed during banking hours and the three clerks were playing poker behind the counter with the bank's money. To give them a fright, he rang the alarm bell three times but none of them moved. However, a few minutes later the barman from the pub across the road brought over three pints of stout.

A Kerryman claimed that Ireland must be the healthiest country in the world.

'Why else,' he asked, 'would the government be closing all the hospitals?'

An Englishman, an Irishman and a Kerryman were stranded on a little island in the middle of the Pacific Ocean and one day they found a magic bottle. When they rubbed it, a genie appeared and granted them each any one wish they desired.

'I'd like to be back in London,' said the Englishman and he was whisked away.

'I'd like to be back in Dublin,' said the Irishman and he too was whisked away.

'I'm very lonely here all on my own,' said the Kerryman, 'I wish my friends were back again.'

☺   ☺   ☺

Two Kerrymen were complaining about how lazy their sons were.

'Look at my fellow, Seán,' said the first, 'he's so lazy he just sits looking at the television all day.'

'So does my fellow, Mick,' said the second, 'but he's too lazy even to switch it on.'

☺   ☺   ☺

A Kerryman got a part in a play where he had only one line to say – 'hark I hear a pistol shot!'

He went around for months beforehand practising his line and driving everybody mad saying: 'hark I hear a pistol shot!'

On the night of the opening performance he came on stage and when the gun went off he shouted: 'What the hell was that noise?'

☺   ☺   ☺

First Kerryman: 'I was reading in a book the other day that we only use a third of our brains.'
Second Kerryman: 'What do we do with the other third?'

☺   ☺   ☺

Two Kerrymen were out flying when their plane caught fire. The first Kerryman bailed out and pulled the cord of his parachute which opened immediately. The second Kerryman jumped out, pulled the cord, but nothing happened. He went zooming towards the ground at high speed past the first Kerryman. The first Kerryman pulled a knife from his pocket and began to cut at his parachute straps shouting: 'right, if you want a race I'll give you one.'

☺   ☺   ☺

Policeman to the Kerryman: 'What's your name?'
Kerryman: 'Happy Birthday to you, Happy Birthday to you, Happy Birthday dear Mick – it's Mick.'

☺   ☺   ☺

A Kerryman was before the court charged with riding a bicycle with no light on.
    'How do you plead?' the judge asked him.
    'Guilty, your honour,' said the Kerryman, 'but insane.'

☺   ☺   ☺

A Kerryman was asked in an interview if he had ever used a dictaphone.
    'No,' he replied, 'I use a telephone like everyone else.'

☺   ☺   ☺

A Kerry stunt driver decided to go for a world record by driving a bus off a ramp over a line of fifty motorbikes. He very nearly made it but halfway across someone rang the bell.

☺ ☺ ☺

A Kerryman was taking an intelligence test.

'What is black,' asked the examiner, 'and is worn on the foot in wet weather?'

'I don't know,' said the Kerryman.

'It's a wellington boot,' said the examiner, 'now think before you answer the next question – what are black and are worn on the feet in wet weather?'

'I don't know,' said the Kerryman.

'It's a pair of wellington boots,' said the examiner, 'now think before you answer the final question – who lives in the White House and rules over millions of Americans?'

'I know that one,' shouted the Kerryman thinking deeply, 'it's three wellington boots.'

☺ ☺ ☺

Sign seen on a road in Kerry:
To make a right turn make three left turns.

☺ ☺ ☺

Have you heard about the twenty-stone Kerryman who went on a seafood diet?

He only had to see food and he'd eat it.

☺ ☺ ☺

There was this Kerryman in a bar who ordered twenty-seven half-pints of stout and drank them down one after the other. 'Why don't you drink pints instead, sir?' asked the barman, 'it would be a lot more convenient.'

'I used to drink pints,' said the Kerryman, 'but the doctor told me they were making me terribly fat, so now I drink half-pints instead.'

☺ ☺ ☺

This fellow was staying on a Kerryman's farm and he couldn't help noticing that one of the pigs had a wooden leg. Naturally he asked the Kerryman why.

'Well,' said the Kerryman, 'that's quite a remarkable pig. One night when we were all asleep, the house caught fire. That pig roused the entire household and saved two of the children single-handedly.

'A few weeks later he was out digging on the land when he discovered oil that's bringing me in a small fortune and recently I've found out that he is working on a new language so that pigs can communicate with human beings.'

'But why the wooden leg?' said the fellow.

'You couldn't eat a pig like that all in one go,' said the Kerryman.

☺ ☺ ☺

One Kerryman called round to see another and was astonished to find his friend's son hammering nails into the furniture.

'Why do you let him do that?' he asked.

'It keeps him out of mischief,' was the reply.

'Isn't it a bit expensive?' asked the first Kerryman.

'No,' said the second, 'not a bit – I get the nails free at work.'

☺ ☺ ☺

This little fellow parked his car in a narrow laneway near a Kerryman's house, so the Kerryman came out and asked him to shift it.

'Why should I?' said the fellow, 'after all it's a cul-de-sac, isn't it?'

'Look,' said the Kerryman, 'I don't care what make it is, shift it.'

☺   ☺   ☺

Have you heard about the Kerry village that was too small to have a village idiot so they all took turns?

☺   ☺   ☺

A Kerryman was out of work so he went around from house to house asking if there were any odd jobs to be done. One fellow felt sorry for him so he gave him a pot of yellow paint and a brush and told him to paint his porch yellow from top to bottom. About an hour later the Kerryman, dripping in paint, came round for his money and said, 'the job is finished, oh, and by the way that's not a Porsche, it's a Mercedes.'

☺   ☺   ☺

A Kerryman went to New York and was driving around in a cab and the cab driver asked him the following riddle – 'Who has the same father and mother as me but is not my brother and not my sister?'

'I don't know,' said the Kerryman.

'It's me,' said the cab driver.

'Begob,' said the Kerryman to himself, 'that's a good one', so when he got home he tried it out on the lads in the pub.

'Who has the same father and mother as me but is not my brother and not my sister?' he asked them.

'We don't know,' they all replied.

'It's a cab driver in New York,' shouted the Kerryman.

☺   ☺   ☺

How do you recognise a Kerryman's dishwasher?
It's all clogged up with paper plates.

☺   ☺   ☺

A Kerryman went into the post office and asked for a licence for his dog.

'Certainly,' said the clerk, 'what's the name?'

'Fido,' said the Kerryman.

☺   ☺   ☺

A Kerryman had his car stolen by a man he thought was his friend and due to a technicality the fellow got off scot free.

'He'll regret it to his dying day,' said the Kerryman, 'if ever he lives that long.'

☺   ☺   ☺

A Kerryman was travelling by train and the ticket collector asked him where he was getting off.

'Killarney,' said the Kerryman.

'That's impossible,' said the ticket collector, 'we don't stop at Killarney on Tuesdays.'

'Look,' said the Kerryman, 'it's very urgent, I must get off at Killarney today.'

'I cannot break the regulations, sir,' said the ticket collector.

'Look,' said the Kerryman, 'it's really very urgent, here's €100, get the driver to slow down a bit and I'll jump off.'

So the ticket collector agreed while warning the Kerryman to keep running after his feet touched the platform or otherwise he would be badly injured.

As the train came into Killarney it slowed to a crawl and the Kerryman jumped off and ran furiously along the platform. As he neared the front of the train a dining carriage attendant grabbed him and pulled him on board saying: 'You're very, very lucky to have made it because we don't stop at Killarney on Tuesdays.'

☺ ☺ ☺

Have you heard about the Kerryman who went fly-fishing? He caught a two-pound fly.

☺ ☺ ☺

Notice in a newspaper inserted by a Kerryman:
'For sale: Twelve donkeys male and female reasonably priced to clear.
P.S. Four of the above have already been sold.'

☺ ☺ ☺

'How is business?' a Kerry trader was asked.

'Terrific,' he replied, 'I bought a tractor for €10,000, traded it for two cars, traded each of them for two motor bikes, traded each of the motorbikes for four racing bicycles and finally sold the racing bicycles for €10,000.'

'But you didn't make a profit.'

'Maybe not,' said the Kerryman, 'but look at all the business I did.'

☺ ☺ ☺

Corkman: 'Do you spend all day going up that ladder?'
Kerryman: 'No, half the time I come down.'

☺ ☺ ☺

A Kerryman lost an arm but always kept his wristwatch on the stump of the arm he had lost.

'Wouldn't it be more convenient to keep it on the good arm?' a friend asked.

'And what would I wind it with?' said the Kerryman.

☺ ☺ ☺

A Kerryman went into a shop and asked for a bottle of sauce.

'Certainly, sir,' said the girl behind the counter, 'would you like HP?'

'No,' said the Kerryman, 'I'm paying cash.'

☺ ☺ ☺

There's a fantastic new restaurant just opened in Kerry. Inside the door there's a big tank of water. The waiter hands you a net and you can choose any steak you want.

☺ ☺ ☺

Foreman: 'I thought you promised me that you would have that work finished this evening.'

Kerryman: 'I'll have it done this evening even if it takes me until tomorrow night.'

☺ ☺ ☺

A Kerryman was an undertaker and one day a wealthy young woman came in to his premises and identified a corpse as her father.

She gave orders for an expensive and elaborate funeral. Just as she was about to leave, the corpse's lower jaw opened and exposed a set of false teeth.

'My father didn't have false teeth,' she then shrieked, 'cancel that order.' The Kerryman took the body out of the expensive coffin and said to it: 'You fool, you'd have had a first-class funeral if only you'd kept your damn mouth shut.'

☺ ☺ ☺

A Kerryman was called up for jury duty and was asked by the judge if he believed in capital punishment.

'I do,' said the Kerryman, 'if it's not too severe.'

Two Kerry businessmen met at Killarney railway station.

'Where are you going?' asked the first.

'Dublin,' said the second.

'You're telling me you're going to Dublin so I'll think you are going to Cork. But I happen to know from another source that you are going to Dublin, so there's no point telling me lies.'

☺ ☺ ☺

A Kerryman's neighbour called to borrow his donkey but the Kerryman told him it was already lent. Just then the donkey brayed loud and clear in his stable.

'But you said your donkey was already lent,' protested the neighbour.

'He is,' said the Kerryman, 'now who are you going to believe – the donkey or me?'

☺ ☺ ☺

A Kerryman was up before the court charged with having his dog driving his car.

'Do you have anything to say in your defence?' asked the judge.

'Nothing,' said the Kerryman, 'except that I once saw a horse talking on television.'

☺ ☺ ☺

A Kerryman was about to be hung for murder when a telegram arrived. The executioner opened the telegram and began to laugh out loud.

'Have I been given a last minute pardon?' asked the Kerryman anxiously.

'No,' laughed the executioner, 'but you've just won €500,000 in the National Lottery.

☺   ☺   ☺

A Kerryman went into a pet shop and told the assistant that he wanted a new mirror for his pet budgie.

'Would you like a large one or a small one, sir?' asked the assistant.

'I don't rightly know,' said the Kerryman.

'Why not bring him into the shop, sir?' said the assistant, 'and we'll try him out in front of a few mirrors and see which one he likes best.'

'That would never do,' said the Kerryman, 'it's for his birthday and I want it to be a surprise.'

☺   ☺   ☺

First Kerryman: 'The trouble with Corkmen is that they have no backbone.'
Second Kerryman: 'They have backbone all right if only they would bring it to the front.'

☺   ☺   ☺

Cork foreman: 'I can lick any Kerryman working for me.'
Brawny Kerryman: 'You can't lick me and I'm a Kerryman that's working for you.'
Cork foreman: 'You're fired.'

☺   ☺   ☺

First Kerryman: 'What do you think of Dubliners?'
Second Kerryman: 'Between you and me, some of them aren't the full fifty percent.'

☺   ☺   ☺

Kerry preacher at a funeral service: 'My dear brothers and sisters, this corpse was a member of our congregation for the last twenty-five years.'

☺   ☺   ☺

A Kerryman was charged with deserting his wife.

'I award your wife €1,000 a month,' said the judge.

'That's very generous of your honour,' said the Kerryman, 'I'll try and give her a few quid myself as well.'

☺   ☺   ☺

Have you heard about the Kerryman who got a job as a public toilet attendant?

They had to let him go because he couldn't remember the prices.

☺   ☺   ☺

A Kerryman got a job as a zoo keeper to one of the world's rarest female gorillas. The gorilla, however, had refused to mate with all the male gorillas that the zoo authorities had flown in from abroad at great expense. In desperation they asked the Kerryman if he would mate with the gorilla for €10,000. He agreed on three conditions:

(i) That the gorilla be given a thorough bath.

(ii) That any offspring resulting from the union be raised as Irish Catholics.

(iii) That he be given a month to raise the €10,000.

A tourist arrived in a Kerry hotel. The porter took his bags and said to him, 'Follow me, sir, I'll be right behind you.'

☺ ☺ ☺

Kerryman: 'I think I need a pair of spectacles.'
Man in white coat: 'You certainly do – this is a fish and chip shop.'

☺ ☺ ☺

Two Kerrymen were out driving together.

'Are we getting near a town?' asked the first.

'We must be,' said the second, 'because we seem to be knocking down more people.'

'Well drive slower then,' said the first.

'What do you mean, drive slower?' said the second, 'you're driving, aren't you?'

☺ ☺ ☺

During a flight from Dublin to London a businessman decided to switch seats. He then found himself seated next to a talkative Kerryman.

'It's nice to meet you,' said the Kerryman, 'did you get on just now?'

☺ ☺ ☺

Have you heard about the Kerryman who was so tall he had to climb a ladder to shave himself?

☺ ☺ ☺

A Kerryman was suffering from BO so his girlfriend advised him to go home, have a bath and afterwards use deodorant and toilet water. Next day she met the Kerryman with his head all covered in bandages.

'What happened?' she asked him.

'The toilet seat hit me on the head,' said the Kerryman.

☺ ☺ ☺

Kerryman to garage proprietor: 'Would you have a truncated, hexagonal gasket for a blue van?'

☺ ☺ ☺

A court case was in session in Dublin where a German sailor had been charged with being drunk and disorderly.

'I cannot understand a word,' said the judge, 'is there anybody in court who can translate what this man is saying?'

'I'm a fluent speaker of German,' said a Kerryman, 'I'll do it.'

'Good,' said the judge, 'ask him what his name is.'

'Vot iss your name?' said the Kerryman.

☺ ☺ ☺

A Kerryman walked into a bar and asked the barman for a pint of less.

'Less?' said the barman, 'I'm not exactly sure if we stock that at the moment. Tell me what exactly is less?'

'I don't know,' said the Kerryman, 'but the doctor told me I would have to drink less from now on.'

☺ ☺ ☺

Kerry Preacher: 'Let us all get on our knees and thank God we are still on our feet.'

☺ ☺ ☺

A Kerryman bought a fantastic new watch for €5 from a street trader. He was very proud of it because it was guaranteed waterproof, shockproof, anti-magnetic, with 237 jewels and accurate to within one millionth of a microsecond per light year. One night the Kerryman was watching television with his wife when the 'News at Ten' came on the screen. The Kerryman looked at his watch and it said half-past eight. He screamed at his wife, 'have you been messing about with the television set again?'

☺   ☺   ☺

A conversation between two Kerrywomen:
    'How is Mick, your husband?'
    'Better, thank God, a lot better.'
    'And how is his diarrhoea?'
    'Thickenin', thank God, thickenin'.'

☺   ☺   ☺

Have you heard about the Kerryman who won a spot prize at a dance?
    He had a total of 4,723 spots.

☺   ☺   ☺

Have you heard about the Kerryman who lost all his teeth? He slept with his head under the pillow and the fairies took them all during the night.

☺   ☺   ☺

Vet: 'Give your cow a tablespoon of this medicine three times a day.'
Kerryman: 'I can't, because the cow doesn't use a tablespoon. She drinks from a bucket.'

Quizmaster: 'Why are cows kept in a pasture?'
Kerryman: 'So they will give pasteurised milk.'

☺   ☺   ☺

A Kerryman went into a hardware store and asked if he could buy a sink.

'Would you like one with a plug, sir?' asked the assistant.

'Don't tell me they've gone electric,' said the Kerryman.

☺   ☺   ☺

Have you heard about the Kerryman who opened a restaurant where people could eat dirt cheap?

It went bust, because people didn't want to eat dirt.

☺   ☺   ☺

Lawyer: 'Do you wish to challenge any member of the jury?'
Kerryman: 'I think I could fight that little fellow on the end.'

☺   ☺   ☺

A policeman knocked on a Kerryman's door and told him a body had just been washed up on the beach and the authorities thought it might be his.

'What did he look like?' asked the Kerryman.

'Well he was about your height and build,' said the policeman.

'And was he wearing serge trousers?' asked the Kerryman, 'because I always wear serge trousers.'

'Actually he was,' said the policeman.

'What colour?' asked the Kerryman.

'Blue,' said the policeman.

'That couldn't have been me,' said the Kerryman, 'because I always wear black serge trousers.'

A rich man hired a Kerrywoman to do his cleaning for him but she failed to give satisfaction. Eventually he had to have a word with her but he tried to put it as gently as possible.

'You know,' Bridget,' he said to her one day, 'I can write my name on the dust on this desk.'

'Can you now, sir?' she replied, 'isn't education a wonderful thing.'

☺ ☺ ☺

A Kerryman asked a Dubliner how he was so smart.

'It's our diet,' said the Dubliner, 'and if you give me €100 I'll sell you some food that will make you smart too.'

'Done,' said the Kerryman, so the Dubliner sold him a pound of Dublin Bay prawns for €100 and the Kerryman ate them. When the Kerryman had bought the third batch of prawns for €100 he said to the Dubliner, 'hold on a minute, I can buy those for €5 a pound in Moore Street.'

'Right,' said the Dubliner, 'just look how smart you're getting already.'

☺ ☺ ☺

A Kerryman got a job with a big firm.

'Here,' said the boss, 'is a brush. Your first task is to sweep the floor.'

'Hold on,' said the Kerryman, 'I'm a university graduate.'

'OK,' said the boss, 'I'll show you how.'

☺ ☺ ☺

Two Kerrymen, a bit worse for drink, awoke in a room in which the blinds were drawn.

'Is it day or night?' asked the first Kerryman.

'I'll go and have a look,' said the second so he went over to the window, lifted the blind and looked out. Then he walked back and lay on his bed.

'Well,' said the first Kerryman, 'is it day or night?'
'I can't remember,' said the second Kerryman.

☺   ☺   ☺

Judge: 'Have you got a competent lawyer to defend you?'
Kerryman: 'No, I haven't, but don't worry about me your honour, because I've got a few good friends on the jury.'

☺   ☺   ☺

A Kerryman walked into a posh restaurant leaving a trail of mud behind him on the expensive carpet.

'Please clean your shoes before entering our establishment,' said a haughty waiter.

'What shoes?' said the Kerryman.

☺   ☺   ☺

A Kerryman called into his bank and told the manager that he had just lost his new cheque book.

'Don't worry though,' he assured the manager, 'they won't be of any use to anybody who finds them because I've signed them all.'

☺   ☺   ☺

What have you got in your pocket?' one Kerryman asked another.

'I'll give you a clue,' said the second, 'it begins with the letter N.'

'A napple,' said the first Kerryman.

'No,' said the second, 'I told you it begins with the letter N.'

'A norange,' said the first Kerryman.

'No, no' said the second, 'I'm telling you for the last time

that it begins with the letter N.'
'Would it be a nonion?' said the first Kerryman.
'You got it at last,' said the second Kerryman.

☺ ☺ ☺

First Kerryman: 'What is that on your leg?'
Second Kerryman: 'A birthmark.'
First Kerryman: 'How long have you had it?'

☺ ☺ ☺

One of the world's richest men had a set of dominoes in which there were huge diamonds instead of spots. One night a Kerryman broke into his house and stole the double blank.

☺ ☺ ☺

One Kerryman met another who was carrying two large suitcases.

'Let me tell you about this fantastic new watch I've got,' said the first. 'It's accurate to a millionth of a microsecond and will tell you the time in Tokyo, San Francisco and Melbourne. It's got a built-in calendar, a calculator and a computer. It can tell you the date of any historical event, the time of the tide in any port of the world and the position of the planets at any time in the next thousand years.'

'That's terrific,' said the second Kerryman, 'tell me, what's in the suitcases?'

'That's the battery,' said the first Kerryman.

☺ ☺ ☺

Have you heard about the new game that is all the rage in Kerry? Two Kerrymen go into a darkened room together and then one of them leaves the room. The other one then tries to guess who left.

Knock knock,
Who's there?
Michael Jackson,
Michael Jackson who?
Frank Sinatra.

☺   ☺   ☺

Two Kerrymen went into an employment agency looking for jobs.

'What can you do?' the first was asked.

'I'm a fully qualified pilot,' said the first.

'Good,' he was told, 'we have vacancies for pilots at the moment.'

'How about you?' the second was asked.

'I'm a woodcutter,' said the second, 'one of the best in the business.'

'Sorry,' was the reply, 'we have no vacancies for wood-cutters at the moment.'

'But,' said the second, 'how can he pile it if there's no one to cut it first?'

☺   ☺   ☺

Corkman: 'Lovely day, isn't it?'
Kerryman: 'I don't know. I'm a stranger here myself.'

☺   ☺   ☺

A Kerryman was asked in an interview what he thought of the American space program.

'I don't know,' he replied, 'I never watch it.'

☺   ☺   ☺

A Kerryman went to America where he became a policeman. One day he was assigned to keep order at a communist parade. Anxious to do his job well, the Kerryman took his baton and hit an innocent spectator who was just looking at the parade. 'What did you do that for?' said the spectator, 'in fact I'm an anti-communist.'

'Look,' said the Kerryman, 'I don't care what sort of communist you are.'

☺   ☺   ☺

The following small ad is said to have appeared in a Kerry newspaper: For sale: A pair of wellingtons. Worn only once – from 1973 to 1984.

☺   ☺   ☺

A Kerryman was asked by a census taker if he had any running water in his house.

'We used to have,' he replied, 'but we had the roof fixed a few years ago.'

☺   ☺   ☺

A Kerryman and his wife set up home in an old railway carriage parked in a siding on a closed branch-line. The Kerryman got lots of exercise pushing the carriage up and down the track every time his wife went to the toilet.

☺   ☺   ☺

A Kerryman took his best suit in to be dry-cleaned. As he was to collect it he happened to notice that there was a large soup stain on the front. When he pointed this out to the assistant she said to him, 'You can't hold us responsible for that. It was there when you brought it in.'

A Kerryman went to the doctor and told him that he got a terrible pain in his arm every time he raised it over his head. 'Don't raise it over your head then,' said the doctor.

☺   ☺   ☺

Two Kerrymen were walking along a golf course when suddenly there was a shout of 'fore' and a golf ball came flying through the air and hit one of them on the head.
'Watch out,' said the other Kerryman throwing himself on the grass, 'there are three more to come.'

☺   ☺   ☺

Two Kerrymen became redundant so they decided to use their redundancy money to set themselves up as painters. The local parish priest asked them to paint the church for him and they offered to do it for €10,000. However, paint proved to be a lot more expensive than they had envisaged and they found their stocks running out before they were even half finished. In desperation they bought gallons of turpentine and added it to their remaining paint and finished the job.

About a month later they called into the church to see how it looked and found large areas of paint peeling from the walls. As they sneaked out of the church they heard a booming voice calling out from above – 'Repaint you thinners.'

☺   ☺   ☺

A Kerryman took an adult education course in mathematics. He thought the teacher was in love with him because she was always putting kisses on his sums.

☺   ☺   ☺

Quizmaster: 'Who was the first woman in the world?'
Kerryman: 'I don't know.'
Quizmaster: 'I'll give you a clue – she had something to do with an apple.'
Kerryman: 'Would it be Granny Smith?'

☺   ☺   ☺

A Kerryman complained to a friend at a dance that nobody would dance with him.

'Look,' said the friend, 'to be brutally honest with you, it's the smell from your socks. Go home, change them and when you come back to the dance you'll have girls falling all over you.'

An hour later they met again and the Kerryman complained that there had been no improvement.

'Did you change your socks like I told you?' asked the friend.

'Of course I did,' said the Kerryman, producing the original pair from his pocket.

☺   ☺   ☺

Have you heard about the Kerryman who had to take a pep-pill every morning to get enough energy to get out of bed so he could go the chemist to buy his tranquillisers?

☺   ☺   ☺

A Kerryman got a job on a submarine but got the sack after only a week. He insisted on sleeping with the windows open.

☺   ☺   ☺

A Kerryman went to the optician's and the assistant asked him if his eyes had ever been checked.

'No,' said the Kerryman, 'they've always been blue.'

During the visit to this part of the solar system of Halley's comet, a Kerryman was asked what he thought of this heavenly wonder. 'It's a sure sign of frost,' he replied.

☺   ☺   ☺

Optician: 'Would you read the letters on this card please?'
Kerryman: 'Would you mind reading it to me, because my sight isn't very good?'

☺   ☺   ☺

A Kerryman went to the doctor and told him he had just swallowed a bone.
   'Are you choking?' the doctor asked him.
   'No,' said the Kerryman, 'I'm serious.'

☺   ☺   ☺

Have you heard about the Kerryman who stood outside a brothel for two hours waiting for the red light to turn green?

☺   ☺   ☺

A little Kerry boy was doing his homework so he asked his father where the pyramids were.
   'I don't know,' said the Kerryman, 'you should remember where you put things.'

☺   ☺   ☺

A Kerryman and his wife were out one evening when burglars broke into their house. They called the police and reported all the things that were missing including jewellery and money.
   'Was there any other damage, sir?' asked a policeman.

'No,' said the Kerryman, 'but we had a pot of Irish stew cooking on the stove and one of them did something disgusting in it. We had to throw half of it away.'

☺   ☺   ☺

Have you heard about the Kerryman who thought that Chanel No. 5 was one of those new satellite television stations?

☺   ☺   ☺

A Kerryman went to his doctor and told him that he had been feeling so depressed an hour previously that he had taken a hundred of the little yellow sleeping tablets that the doctor had prescribed for him the week before. Now he regretted his decision to commit suicide and asked the doctor to save him.

'Don't worry,' said the doctor, 'those were not sleeping tablets, they were laxatives.'

☺   ☺   ☺

A Dubliner, a Corkman and a Kerryman each tendered for a big construction job in England, paid for by government money.

'I'll do it for €20,000,' said the Kerryman.

'How is that figure broken down?' asked the boss of the construction company.

€10,000 for the materials and €10,000 for labour,' said the Kerryman.

'I'll do it for €40,000,' said the Dubliner, 'that's €20,000 for the materials and €20,000 for labour.'

'Look,' said the Corkman, 'my tender is for €60,000. That's €20,000 for you, €20,000 for me and we'll give the other €20,000 to the Kerryman to do the job.'

Have you heard about the Kerryman who was upstairs guarding his money when two other Kerrymen broke in downstairs and watched television?

Three carpenters, an Englishman, an Irishman and a Kerryman were boasting about the high degree of accuracy they used in their work.

'We have to work to the nearest hundredth of an inch,' said the Englishman.

'We have to work to the nearest thousandth of an inch,' said the Irishman.

'That wouldn't do us at all,' smiled the Kerryman, 'we have to get it dead right.'

☺   ☺   ☺

A sophisticated Kerryman was advising his younger brother who was just about to make a trip up the world's longest one-way street – the road from Kerry to Dublin.

'Those fellows up in Dublin,' he told him, 'humour them, agree with them. Even if they say that Dublin is bigger than Tralee, agree with them.'

☺   ☺   ☺

A Kerryman was working on a building site and one day the foreman told him to go down a deep pit. The Kerryman stepped into the pit and fell thirty feet to the bottom.

'Why didn't you use the ladder?' shouted the foreman.

'I thought that was for coming up,' groaned the Kerryman.

☺   ☺   ☺

Have you heard about the Kerryman who invented the first telephone?

He had to wait twenty years for someone to invent the second telephone. Then when he rang him up he found it was engaged.

Then there was the Kerryman who applied for a half-price television licence because he had only one eye.

☺ ☺ ☺

Doctor: 'You have been very badly injured in an accident. Please tell me your name so I can inform your wife.'
Kerryman: 'There's no need to. My wife already knows my name.'

☺ ☺ ☺

Have you heard about the Kerryman and his wife who were in the steel and iron business?

He did the stealing and she did the ironing.

☺ ☺ ☺

A Kerryman emigrated to England because he was told that the streets there were paved with gold and that all you had to do was to bend down and pick it up. As he got off the train in London on Saturday night he saw a five pound note lying on the platform so he bent down and picked it up. As he was just about to put it into his pocket he suddenly threw it away saying, 'I won't start until Monday.'

☺ ☺ ☺

An old Kerryman was asked if he was in America during the Wall Street Crash.

'Of course I was,' he replied, 'didn't it nearly fall on top of me.'

☺ ☺ ☺

This fellow hired a Kerryman to put in concealed lighting in his exclusive new house.

The Kerryman papered over all the switches.

☺ ☺ ☺

A Kerryman was dancing with a girl at a ceilí when she asked him if he knew 'The Walls of Limerick'.

'Know them?' said the Kerryman, 'wasn't my sister married to one of them.'

A Kerryman was sending his young fellow down to the shop to buy some provisions.

'Get ten kilograms of spuds,' he told him, 'but don't get any big ones because they're too heavy to carry.'

☺ ☺ ☺

Two Kerrymen were working on a building site and one day the first Kerryman's wife arrived to see him while he was climbing up a ladder with half a ton of blocks on his back.

'Don't turn round,' said the second Kerryman, 'but look who's behind you.'

☺ ☺ ☺

A Kerryman was complaining to a neighbour about the high cost of food.

'It's not like the old days,' he said to him, 'when you could make a meal out of nothing if you had the stuff.'

☺ ☺ ☺

A Kerryman was missing for two weeks so his wife informed the police. One morning they knocked on her door and said that her husband's body had been found floating in a canal.

'Yerra, that couldn't be him,' she told them, 'because he could not swim.'